Dog Training
FOR KIDS

by
CAROL LEA BENJAMIN

Illustrations by the author

Photographs by Charles Wiesehahn

Second Edition

**HOWELL
BOOK HOUSE**
New York

Howell Book House
Macmillan Publishing Company
866 Third Avenue, New York, NY 10022
Collier Macmillan Canada, Inc.

Library of Congress Cataloging-in-Publication Data

Benjamin, Carol Lea.
   Dog training for kids

   Summary: Easy-to-follow instructions on training
and handling a dog.
   1. Dogs—Training—Juvenile literature [1. Dogs—
Training] I. Wiesehahn, Charles, ill. II. Title.
SF431.B42   1988   636.7'0887   87-26297
ISBN 0-87605-541-2

Macmillan books are available at special discounts for bulk purchases
for sales promotions, premiums, fund-raising, or educational use.
For details, contact:

        Special Sales Director
        Macmillan Publishing Company
        866 Third Avenue
        New York, NY 10022

10 9 8 7 6 5 4

Printed in the United States of America

To Fred Healy

with a hug and a kiss
for Bill Scolnik and Rick Tomita

Contents

About the Author

After graduating from college, Carol Lea Benjamin worked as a detective, an editor, a teacher and then a dog trainer.

Dog Training for Kids, winner of the Dog Writers' Association of America Award as Best Children's Book of the Year when it was first published in 1976, now newly revised and expanded, was her first book, a perfect blend of her talents as a teacher and as a professional dog trainer.

Since then, she has written many books for children and adults, including *Cartooning for Kids, Writing for Kids, Running Basics, Dog Problems, Dog Tricks, Mother Knows Best: the Natural Way to Train Your Dog* and two novels, *The Wicked Stepdog* and *Nobody's Baby Now.*

Carol Lea Benjamin's children's books have twice received starred reviews in *The School Library Journal,* have twice been selected among Children's Books of the Year by Bank Street College and have been well reviewed widely, including in the *New York Times,* the *Los Angeles Times, Saturday Review* and *Newsweek.*

As a dog writer, Carol Benjamin is very highly regarded. In 1985 she was named Writer of the Year by the Dog Writers' Association of America and in that same year she was voted Dogdom's Writer of the Year, making her a winner of the prestigious Fido Award.

Her articles have appeared in *Time, Better Homes and Gardens, Medical Economics, Private Practice, Apartment Life, Off-Lead, Runners World, The German Shepherd Dog Review, Animals* and many others. She is an international advisor to *Dogs U*S*A* and writes a monthly column, Dog Trainer's Diary, for *Pure-bred Dogs—American Kennel Gazette,* the official publication of the American Kennel Club. She has also had numerous appearances on radio, television and for kennel clubs as an expert on dog behavior.

Ms. Benjamin is a member of the Authors' Guild and the Dog Writers' Association of America.

Carol Benjamin lives in New York City with her husband, architect Stephen Lennard, and their dogs, Scarlet, a German Shepherd, and Lefty, a Japanese Shiba Inu.

Introduction:
It's Great to Have a Dog for a Friend

Dogs are warm, loyal and fun-loving. They forgive all your faults in advance. Who else but a dog will pounce on you with welcoming love when all you did was step out for the mail? And who else but a dog will spend a week at the foot of your bed when you have the flu? The care a dog needs seems such a small price to pay for all the devotion you get in return.

Many pure-breds and mixed breed dogs are good with kids and easy to train. The pictures in this book show several different breeds that are good with kids, but there are lots more. Every kind of dog can and should be trained. As you read on, you'll see what a few of them look like while they are working and goofing off.

All the dogs insisted on having their names printed in the book, so there is a list in the back of who everyone is. Some of them were hoping for fan letters, but don't waste your time. Only three of them can read, and not too well at that.

Most dogs are pretty good listeners!

Dog Sense

The cutest puppy that ever was born.

IF YOUR DOG GOOFS . . .

like this . . .

or like this . . .

or like this . . .

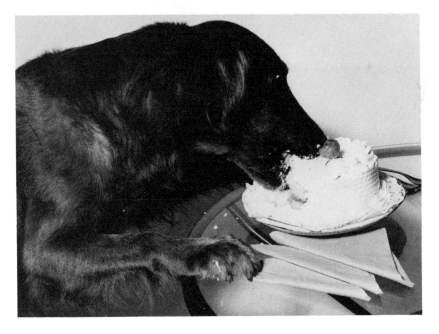

or like this . . .

or like this . . .

or like this . . .

—you need help in training him!

WHY TRAIN YOUR DOG?

If your dog could read, he'd probably buy you this book himself. Then he'd know that training is the key he needs to unlock the dog house. Trained, he could go anywhere with you. If he stayed home, he'd have the run of the house. He could help you wow your friends and family with snappy tricks. Maybe he'd even win some trophies and ribbons at obedience trials. He wouldn't feel like an unruly, rejected klutz any more. He'd be self-confident and clever, knowing how to behave in all situations. It's easy to see that a trained dog is a happier dog.

Once he's trained, you'll be so proud of him! Why not? No longer will he jump up on Aunt Betty with his muddy paws. Never, never will he steal the birthday cake and devour it, candles and all, while "Happy Birthday" is being sung. No more will he trip you on the stairs or try to pull you across a crowded street because he's spied a cat. And finally, there'll be an end to unsightly accidents on the living room carpet. Now he'll stand still while you brush him and make him look his best. He'll come when you call him. He'll stay put at your command, at home, outdoors and even in the family car. He'll walk contentedly at your side. He won't dash off without a moment's notice, leaving you and your packages flying.

And yet, he'll still roughhouse like any other dog, lick ice cream off your face, fetch a stick and act zany when it snows. He'll be just as goofy and lovable as ever, but controllable when necessary and somewhat better mannered all the time. He'll have more spirit than you ever dreamed possible because he'll be out with you having fun instead of being locked up at home. And because of his training, he'll be smarter and have a greater ability to concentrate on work, on play and on you, his master.

He'll stand still while you brush him.

Trained, he could go anywhere.

A trained dog is a happier dog.

FIRST THINGS FIRST

A Name for Your Puppy

When I was a kid, my dad told me about two dogs he met called Get Off The Rug and You, Too. Some people name their dogs silly names, just for the fun of it. Other people try to suit the dog's personality or to use a name they think is beautiful. One of the loveliest dog names I ever heard belongs to a big mutt who lives right on the Hudson River. Like the fellow creatures that surround his yard, he is called Seagull. And I am hoping one day for a lady dog to name Jasmine, because I love the sound of that word. A dog's name can even be a clue to why his owner got him. Do you think that someone would treat Fang the same way they'd treat Pee Wee or Baby? Whether you go serious or silly, choose a name you love for your new dog. You'll be using it and hearing it a lot.

Since the dog getting housebroken, trained and loved in this book needs a name like any other dog, I named him Pastrami, because I'm always hungry. Pastrami is really your dog. You can even think of your dog's name instead if you like.

Puppy Care

The day your new puppy arrives will be a very exciting day for both of you. To make things smoother, prepare for Pastrami's homecoming before he gets there. Consult your parents and choose a room where he will live until he is well mannered enough to have the run of the house. The kitchen is best during the day. The floor is easy to clean, just in case, and he'll have lots of company because everyone hangs out where the food is.

You can make Pastrami a bed from a cardboard box. An old towel makes nice bedding because it can be washed—and it should be, at least once a week. The box is light so you can move it to your room at night, if that's okay with your parents. Since dogs are "pack animals," they are "programmed" to live in groups. They do not like to be alone. Sleeping in your room will give your puppy the company he needs in order to feel secure all night long.

A better way to make a little house for your dog, one that is also light enough to move from room to room, is to buy him a dog crate, a little, wire cage made for dogs. This crate will become his den—his home, his bed, the place he goes when he wants to rest or chew a rawhide bone. It is a place where he'll be safe when you can't keep an eye on him. It is a place where you can keep him for a few hours at a time when no one can watch him to make sure he doesn't chew the furniture or people's shoes. Puppies will chew anything they can get their mouths around, including your toes. While the crate costs more than a cardboard box, in the long run it can save a fortune—a couch, piano legs, the living room rug, your best running shoes, the plants, etc. Try to get one. It is the most important tool available in raising puppies.

Pastrami will also need a leash and collar. A hook near the front door would be a safe place to hang the leash and collar. Then everyone will know where to find it when it's time to walk Pastrami.

Your puppy will need two dishes. Stainless steel, flat-bottomed bowls are good. They don't break, chip or peel, Pastrami won't be able to chew them up and they are difficult to tip over. They are easy to clean and can even go right in the dishwasher. One dish will be Pastrami's dinner bowl, the other his water dish. Puppies and grown dogs, too, need a daily supply of fresh water.

Every puppy will need a checkup and shots. Take Pastrami to the veterinarian as soon as you can. He will make sure your puppy is healthy and give him the inoculations he needs to prevent common and dangerous diseases. He can also advise you on what to feed Pastrami, how much and how often. He will be familiar with your puppy's growth rate as well as with local brands of dog food. Feel free to ask him questions. He'll be happy to help you keep your puppy in sound condition.

Pastrami will need his own brush, perhaps a comb, and a nail clipper. Many dogs don't need daily grooming to look their best, but brushing a pup will make him *feel* good. A few minutes of brushing

Wet him and soap him from the neck down.

Do his face and ears gently with a wash cloth.

19

every day will keep Pastrami's coat in good condition and minimize the amount of hair that needs to be vacuumed up.

Nail cutting is a little tricky because there is a vein in the nail. When the nails are neglected for months and grow too long, the vein grows longer, too. Then if you clip Pastrami's nails, you might hurt him. Take the nail clipper to the veterinarian on your first visit and ask him or her to show you how to cut your puppy's nails. If Pastrami gets used to nail care when he is young, he won't fight you when he's older and weighs two thousand pounds. Also, check your pup's feet about once a week. If you ran around barefooted all the time, you might get cuts and bruises more often. Look for ticks, scrapes or cuts that might need your attention or the veterinarian's.

Your puppy won't need to bathe as often as you have to. And don't think he doesn't appreciate that. Bathe Pastrami only when he looks, smells or feels dirty. That would be about once a month, unless he meets a skunk in between. Don't overdo baths. They could dry out the dog's skin if he has them too often. But don't forget to bathe him either. That would make him feel all itchy and gross.

When you bathe Pastrami, be careful of his eyes and nose. It's safest to wet him and soap him from the neck down and do his face and ears with a plain, wet washcloth. Rinse well or he'll bubble up when it rains. Dry him with a big towel and duck when he shakes. Just like you, he should stay indoors for a while after his bath unless it is really hot outside. If you've got a camera, now's the time to use it. He'll probably be dirty again in an hour!

Everybody and his uncle is going to want to play with Pastrami because he's surely the cutest puppy that was ever born. Be certain he's well supported at both ends when he's picked up. Place one hand firmly under his bottom and the other on his chest. He'll love the attention and affection, especially when it's coming from you. But he also needs some time alone to rest and sleep and grow and write letters home to his mother. When he needs to rest, he may go into his crate. Or you can put him there. Everybody needs some privacy, even little Pastrami.

Tips and Reminders about Dog Care

1. In the winter, whenever you take your puppy out after the snow, watch out for the salt used to melt it. It can irritate a dog's feet. If you can't avoid walking on it, wash your dog's feet with warm water after every walk.

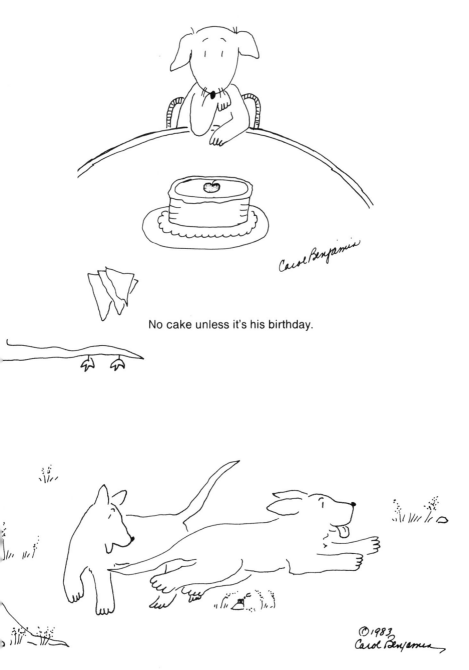

No cake unless it's his birthday.

He needs exercise in the fresh air.

"Puppies do not like to be alone."

2. If your dog's skin gets dry, he may need more fat in his diet. Call your veterinarian and ask him to recommend something. No one wants a dog to have dandruff.
3. Never feed Pastrami chicken bones, steak bones, pork or lamb bones or any bone with sharp edges. And don't feed Pastrami pastrami. It's too spicy.
4. No cake, ice cream or candy unless it's his birthday.
5. Don't feed your dog before going on a long car ride. Wait until you get back home or to your destination if you are staying overnight.
6. Remember that your dog needs a lot of the same things you do—love and affection; an education; companionship; a warm, dry place to sleep; good nutrition; a few possessions to call his own; exercise in the fresh air; and a few rules and regulations to help him feel secure. He counts on you, his kid, for all these things.

Teaching Your Puppy to Stay Alone

The first big hurdle for Pastrami is learning to stay alone. You can expect him to complain a little his first night away from his mother and his brothers and sisters. But if he's in his crate or box, sleeping on a soft towel, with a chew toy available and he's in your room, he shouldn't cry much. He may wake you once or twice the first night. If he does, you can go to him and check to make sure he's okay, but don't take him into bed with you. If you do, he'll always howl to sleep with you—even when he's got fleas. He will settle down, in his crate, and go back to sleep. And after a night or two, it will be as if he were always there, in his little den in your big room.

During the day, Pastrami must practice staying alone. After all, people can't be with him every minute of the day. Before you leave him, make sure he's had food, water and a walk. Make sure his towel is clean and dry. See that he has a safe chew toy. Then let him stay alone in his crate in the kitchen, but only for short periods of time at first. He might carry on the first few times you leave him. That's normal. How does he know you'll ever come back? He can only learn this by experience. So don't go right back and take him out. Wait a few minutes and then go, increasing the time each time you practice. This way, he'll learn to be by himself and to do it quietly. If he makes a racket while he's still learning this important lesson, bang on the

door and say "No!" Soon enough, he'll understand that when you leave, you also return. *Then* he'll be a good dog when he's left alone.

Housebreaking Your Puppy

Housebreaking your puppy may not be your favorite job, but it's a fact of life. We all had to be housebroken at one time or another. So let's keep it simple and do it as efficiently as possible. Just make sure you remember the two prime rules: (1) until the job is finished, no run of the house for him, and (2) no walking barefooted for you.

Some people start by paper training their puppies. But if Pastrami's had his shots, it's not too cold out and you're not gone all day at school, you can housebreak your puppy right to the great outdoors. It will save a lot of time and icky cleanups. Walk him first thing when you get up, before and after all his meals, before playing with him, whenever you see him sniffing or circling and last thing before you go to bed. Be alert. It will save time and work. When you cannot watch him, keep him in his crate.

When Pastrami attends to his needs outside, praise him lavishly. When he goofs, show him his mistake, tell him "No!" and take him right outside to where he should go. Do not rub his nose in his "accident" and do not spank him. This harsh treatment isn't necessary. Most of all, do not call him when he's goofed and you want to correct him. That will make him not want to come when called. Go and get him instead, lead him to the scene of his crime, bang on the floor near the "accident" so that he looks at it, tell him "No, Bad dog" and then take him right outside. There, whether he goes or not, praise him. He'll get it. He's a smart dog, our Pastrami.

Every time Pastrami goes in the right place, outside, and you praise him, you move ahead one giant step. Every time he goofs and you correct him, you move ahead as well. Dogs learn from both praise and correction. Some people think you cannot correct a dog if you don't catch him in the act. But if there is *evidence,* and there always is with a housebreaking mishap, you can correct the dog. Even if his little brain does not remember that he was naughty, his remarkable nose will tell him the mess is his.

Use the crate to confine Pastrami after you feed him, walk him and play with him. Make sure his schedule is humane: out every four hours for very young puppies. Praise him when he gets it right and correct him when he gets it wrong. And be vigilant about his habits.

Praise him lavishly when he's good.

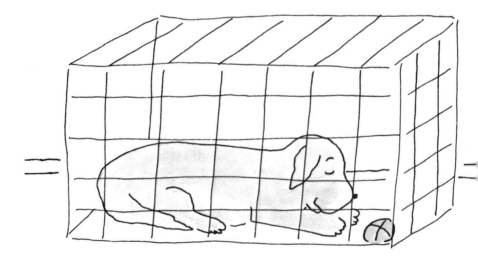

His little den.

These things will get this job done in no time. By the time your puppy is six months old, he will be thoroughly and reliably housetrained.

Sometimes it's not possible to housebreak a puppy directly to the outdoors. If it is sleeting out when Pastrami comes home, or if you go straight from school to football practice or synchronized swimming, you'll have to paper train him first.

Block off an area for the puppy and cover the whole area with newspapers. When he goes on the papers, praise him. Gradually make the papered area smaller, cleaning up all the soiled papers but one. Save one wet paper and put it on the clean ones. The scent will "trigger" your puppy to use that same area again. You can use the wet paper "trigger" technique until he only needs a small area to be covered with paper and he is not making mistakes.

You can still use the crate and a schedule when you are home. But if you are gone all day and no one else is there to take the puppy out, leave the crate door open during the day so that Pastrami can get to his papers. He will eat and sleep in the clean area in and near the crate and relieve himself on the paper.

When Pastrami gets a little older (don't wait too long), and the snows have melted, take a wet paper he has used out with you and put it near the curb to give him the idea of where to go. It may take a few tries and some long walks, but eventually he will go outside. Praise him like crazy and you will be well on your way to having a housebroken pup. From here on, you can proceed with the crate and schedule, removing all the paper for good.

Of course, no matter how watchful you are and how brilliant Pastrami is, sometimes he will goof during the training period and, your luck, he'll do it on the rug. Now, you must make sure that wherever he goofs, you clean up really well to prevent the "trigger" technique from working where you don't want it to.

That's about all there is to housebreaking. Remember:

- Lots of praise when he gets it right.
- No run of the house until he is completely reliable.
- Keep him on a schedule he can predict for his walks. (He must know how long he has to wait or he just won't.)
- Be fair to the family and clean up after him quickly when he does have an accident. (And don't forget to wash your hands before you pick up this book again.)

Leash Training

Very soon after you get him, Pastrami has to get used to wearing a collar and leash. Start with a soft, leather puppy collar and a light leash. First let him wear the collar for a brief period each day while you are at home. Praise him when you put it on him so he associates it with good feelings. After a week or so, clip on the leash and trail after him. Let him go where he likes, just getting used to this new, slight restriction. Little by little, encourage him to go in your direction. Call him sweetly to you—after all, he's still a baby. And whatever you do, do not get into a tug-of-war with him. Instead, coax him along. Take turns leading each other. Soon enough, he'll become accustomed to the leash and begin to trot along near you, sometimes ahead, sometimes out to the side, sometimes stopping to sniff or sit down and think about life.

One important reminder: Pastrami is young and growing like a weed. So check the fit of his collar once a week. If you can comfortably slip two fingers in it, it's still big enough. If doing that makes it tight, skip buying yourself ice cream this week and buy him a new collar.

Good Manners

Every puppy needs to learn the rules of the house. He shouldn't beg at the table. Don't encourage him with tidbits. He must stay off the furniture. Don't invite him up. Tell him "No" if he decides he likes the easy chair better than the floor. He may look cute up there at three months old, but he's growing.

Dog owners and trainers agree that the most important thing you will ever teach your dog is to come when called. If you always make Pastrami glad he came to you, you will be laying a constructive foundation for this command. Therefore, if you ever have to scold or correct your puppy, go and get him. Never call him to you and punish him. That would make him not want to come the next time you call him. Always praise him when he comes. Crouch down and hold your arms out, calling him to you. When he first toddles toward you on his chubby puppy legs, make him happy he did and continue to show pleasure when he comes from then on. It is the best way to insure solid obedience of this command later on.

He'll walk contentedly at your side.

He'll come when you call him.

If Pastrami lived in the wild, he would have to defend his food to survive. But he has you to provide for him and make sure he gets enough to eat every day. So he has no need for this possibly dangerous instinct. The notion that he can and should defend his food could cause him to growl or snap at you. A dog must never, ever show aggression toward anyone in his own family. So, for safety's sake, you should teach him to give up his food when asked. Teach him this lesson when he's young and you'll never have that serious confrontation in the future. Here's how.

When you feed little Pastrami, tell him "OK"—even when it's only a dog biscuit. Once he's used to that, after about a week, show him a biscuit and say "No." Do not let him grab it. If he seems to understand, in other words, if he waits, tell him "OK" and give him the biscuit. Now try once more. This time, after you say "No," put the biscuit on the floor. But you've got to be vigilant and quick. If he goes for it, you've got to beat him to it. If he drools (he will) but resists the biscuit, say "OK" and give it to him with big, big praise.

Continue saying "OK" when you give Pastrami his dinner bowl or hand him a biscuit, but do not practice "No" again for at least a week. Once he understands "No" and "OK," every now and then, but no more than once a week, say "No" while he is eating and take his bowl away. If he doesn't object, add a treat to the bowl and give it right back to him, saying "OK" as you do. If he growls or snaps when you reach for the bowl, tell him "No" in an angry voice and do not give him back the dish for one hour. These lessons, taught early, do more than prevent senseless aggression. They also establish you as boss. As you continue reading, you'll see why this is so important.

But first, a word of warning. Some people think if a little is good, a lot must be better. They badger their little puppies with "No" and "OK" all day long, giving the pup a meal or a bone, then taking it away a moment later. You can make a dog crazy that way, never letting him feel he can keep what's his. If you practice *lightly,* this exercise teaches the puppy that you are in charge, that you will supply his food, as well as his other needs, and that you have the right to monitor what he eats, but you will be kind and fair about it. Any puppy can accept that. So remember, when it comes to teaching your puppy not to protect his food, less is more.

You'll also want to get Pastrami used to the family car and teach him car manners at the same time. He should never ride in the front seat. He could interfere with the driver and that isn't safe. Teach him to sit on one side in the back and not hop around or make noise. Tell him, "Pastrami, get in the car," when you put him in the car. Later, he'll do it on his own when told. When he's older, he'll learn the command to stay and should be told "Stay" before the car door is opened. For safety's sake, he must learn to wait until you are ready to take him out. For now, make sure his leash is on and you are holding it before you open the door. No bounding out and running off for this precious puppy.

Of course, if you have a puppy crate and a station wagon or four-wheel drive vehicle, the safest way to travel with a dog is to put the crate in the car and the puppy in the crate. Then you can leave windows open without worrying about the puppy jumping out. And you don't have to worry so much about doors opening and the puppy doing an escape act. But with or without the crate, you must be very careful about leaving the puppy alone in the car. If it's cool out, you could leave the windows open a crack on each side and let him stay in the car while you and your parents do an errand, providing the place you are leaving him is safe. But never, never leave a dog in a car in hot weather. Cars heat up quickly when they are not moving and dogs are less efficient than humans in cooling their own bodies. Humans sweat through their skin. Dogs do not. They can only cool themselves by sweating through the pads of their feet and by panting. So a hot car can be fatal to a dog in no time.

When you travel with your puppy, take his bowl along and possibly the towel from his crate or bed so that he feels at home. If you are going far, take a bottle of the water he is used to drinking. Some dogs get diarrhea from drinking water they are not used to. Stop when you can and exercise him, too. It's good for both of you on any long drive.

Raising a puppy is a lot of work but it's also a time full of excitement and sweetness. Soon you'll forget the soggy newspapers and your chewed sneaker. But years from now you'll smile at the memory of those soggy kisses, of all the love you got from and gave to your warm, clumsy, silly new friend. What you do now will determine the future character of your dog. With patience and intelligence you can raise a dog to be proud of and love.

Teach him "Go to your bed."

WHAT YOUR DOG WILL LEARN

Here's a quick, exciting coming attraction of Pastrami after training. When you say, "Pastrami, heel," he will walk at your left side, even with your body and at your speed. If you run, he will run. If you walk, he will walk at the same pace. When you stop, he will sit without being told. He will also sit when you say "Sit," lie down when you say "Down," and stand when you say "Stand." He will remain where he is or *freeze* in any of these three positions when you tell him "Stay."

When you call to him, "Pastrami, Come," he will come and automatically sit in front of and facing you. If you then tell him to heel, he will walk to the heeling position at your left side and once again sit without even being asked. He will have a fair sized vocabulary, for a dog, including not only the above commands, but also words and phrases like: No, OK, No jumping, No chewing, No sniff, Quiet, Speak, Go home, Get in the car, Go to your bed and others. He will also understand and respond to several hand signals, which may later be used without voice commands.

He will chew what's his and not what's yours. He will not greet people by knocking them over. He may bark a warning when someone's approaching, but he won't bark for deafening hours just for the fun of it. And if you're very ambitious, he will give his paw, jump through a hoop, play dead, bark and wag his tail on command, take food from your mouth without even chomping on your lips and he might even do the best trick in the world. He'll be impressive to see, our Pastrami, and fun to be with. And all the credit will reflect on you, you lucky kid, so let's get to work and make it happen.

To make the collar, hold one ring and slip the chain through it.

This collar is on the right way.

This collar is on wrong.

34

WHAT YOU NEED AND HOW TO USE IT

All the equipment you need for dog training is a six-foot leather or cotton canvas leash and a slip collar or choke chain. A nylon leash might work for you if your dog is small, but nylon tends to burn the hand and a chain leash would really hurt you if Pastrami forgot his manners and pulled. Even the nicest dog in the world will forget himself *sometimes*.

During training, Pastrami will walk at your left side. The leash will cross in front of you and is carried folded up, waist high, in your right hand. Do not wrap the leash around your hand or you might get hurt. If your dog needs extra holding onto, use two hands.

A slip collar or choke chain is a length of chain with a ring on each end. For size, measure Pastrami's neck and add two inches. To make the chain into a collar, hold one ring and slip the chain through it. There is a trick that will help you to understand the collar and learn how to put it on your dog. Pretend your left arm is your dog's neck (remember that he's going to be at your left side). Slip the chain through one of the rings and slide the loop you have made over your arm so that the ring that pulls it tight (the ring to which you attach the leash) comes toward you from *over* your arm and not under it. Pull and release. The collar will loosen by itself when you stop pulling. Now try it the wrong way. Take it off, turn it around and put it back on your left arm. This time the part you pull comes from underneath. Pull and release. Notice that the collar does not let go. In the next section, How Your Dog Learns, you will learn why it is essential to your dog's learning for the collar to release.

One more word about dog collars. If you are not so big and your dog is, by all means start out with a metal slip collar. But if you can handle the dog on a nylon slip collar, do so. Or if your dog is tiny now or tiny and staying so, use a nylon slip collar or even a flat or rolled leather collar. Never use more equipment or force than you need to control your dog. And remember that the slip collar is a *training collar*. Your dog should only wear it when he is being trained or taken for a walk. His leather collar is much safer for all other times.

The wrong way to hold a leash.

The leash crosses in front of you and is carried in your right hand.

Don't train your dog when you're hungry or grouchy.

Now you are all set to begin training. The only other thing you need is a roast beef sandwich. The roast beef sandwich is not for Pastrami. Never mix food and obedience training. One day you'll be out of food and out of luck. Don't put the choke chain on the sandwich. Roast beef sandwiches are stubborn and difficult to train. Eat the sandwich. Ahhhhh. Now you won't be hungry, grouchy and impatient while training your dog. You're on your way to becoming a good dog trainer.

He shouldn't beg at the table.

Bosco watched jealously.

Never use more equipment than you need to control your dog.

HOW YOUR DOG LEARNS

You cannot reason with your dog. He has the brain power, but not the language. You can observe dogs using reason, but I have yet to hear one speaking English.

One day I was watching my dogs messing around in the kitchen. Oliver began playing with a tennis ball. Bosco watched jealously. Suddenly Bosco left the room. Soon he returned with his rawhide bone. He growled and tossed it around and made a big deal of it. Of course, Oliver got interested. Bosco ignored him and continued prancing with his bone. Oliver could no longer resist. He dropped the tennis ball and went toward Bosco. Bosco immediately dropped the bone, grabbed the tennis ball and made a speedy exit. He certainly had used his brains to get what he wanted. But even though a dog is capable of reason, you and he don't have a common language. So you can't say to him, "See here, Pastrami, if you don't sit when I tell you to, there'll be no TV tonight." A dog learns his lessons mostly through corrections and praise.

Correcting Your Dog

A correction is something you do to your dog when he makes a mistake. It is usually a combination of a quick jerk and release of the leash and a command. Pastrami won't like the correction because your voice will be angry instead of friendly and the jerk on the leash will make the collar tighten for a moment and give him a little pinch around his neck. Cleverly, he'll discover that if he avoids that mistake, no pinch, no yell. Just like you and me, he may need a few corrections to learn his lesson. And don't we all deserve patience while we're learning?

A verbal correction may be used alone if Pastrami is far away from you. Suppose as you walk into the living room you see Pastrami sitting on the couch counting his fleas. Immediately yell "No," run to him saying "Shame, Bad dog!" and drag him off the couch saying "Off." Here you used the verbal correction alone first and then you used it with a physical correction, dragging him off the couch. Well done! Pastrami can count his fleas on the floor and you can start saving up for a new couch.

The correction is one of the keys to effective dog training. Here are some important things to learn about corrections before you begin training Pastrami.

1. Always check to make sure you put the slip collar on correctly before you begin to work. If it is on backwards, it will not release. Pastrami doesn't learn by being choked. He must associate a tight collar with a mistake, not with every minute of training.
2. Tell your dog why you are making a correction every time you make one. Be clear.
3. Be fair. Make sure Pastrami knows what is expected of him.
4. Act angry when Pastrami does something wrong, but inside remain your same patient, sweet self. Don't train the dog the day they give out report cards.
5. Never laugh at a dog's mistakes.

Now let's see what happens to Pastrami when he's a good dog. (By the way, don't let your parents read about corrections. They might get some dangerous ideas!)

Praising Your Dog

Let's face it. We all like to think our dogs would behave just like Lassie and do everything right just because they love us. But it just isn't true. Now that you have learned about corrections, Pastrami will begin to do as you say to avoid them. But if that's all school were about, he'd be a pretty sad sack. He loves you and he wants to please you. He wants your affection and approval very much. So when he does his lessons well, praise him. Never praise him when he is doing something wrong or naughty or he will do it over and over again to get your praise. Praise him when he does something right. Talk to him and pet him. Now's the time to be warm and friendly. Really let him know you appreciate his hard work and you love him. It's best, though, not to praise for too long in the middle of a lesson. It will tend to make him wild and foolish. A couple of nice pats and a warm "Good dog" will do.

After the lesson, you can go to town. Kiss him, roll on the floor with him, go nuts. Praising is what makes the lesson fun for your dog. It can make the difference between a mopey student and a jolly worker who loves to show his stuff.

Never laugh at a dog's mistakes.

After the lesson, kiss him, roll
on the floor with him, go nuts.

You are going to become leader of the pack!

©Carol Benjamin 1983

WHY YOUR DOG LEARNS

Did you ever try to walk a cat on a leash or teach it to lie down on command? It would be a pretty tough and frustrating job. Dogs and cats are very different. It's not only that cats meow instead of barking or prefer fish to knuckle bones. Cats are loners and dogs, like their wild relatives, the wolves, are pack animals. This means that each dog will either have a pack leader or be one. Since dogs are domesticated animals, the family group becomes the pack. And someone in the family will be seen as the pack leader by the dog. This, in fact, is the very reason why your dog can and will learn from you—because you are going to become leader of the pack.

It makes sense for you to become top dog or *alpha* to your dog since you will be training him. And if nobody asserted himself over the dog, he might try to gain the position of top dog for himself. This could be the cause of a lot of trouble. No one tells the boss what to do. Pastrami could feel that you had no right to interfere with his will or his desires. This unfortunate error in dog handling is the cause of a lot of aggression and biting. And it is all unnecessary.

An understanding of your dog's nature as a pack animal enables you to benefit from his instinctive behavior rather than become bullied by a spoiled dog with illusions of importance. Training your dog lovingly but firmly helps establish *you* as top dog. And, strange as it sounds, this is the most important reason of all for training your dog. Therefore, and because you'd look pretty silly on the wrong end of a leash, here is a little primer on how to become alpha. Be sure to share these tips with your family because all the humans in your "pack" should be alpha to all the dogs.

HOW TO BECOME TOP DOG

1. Obedience train your dog.

2. Always praise your dog warmly for obeying a command and for any other good behavior.

3. Always correct your dog fairly and swiftly when he is disobedient or naughty. Forgive quickly.

4. When working with your dog, stand up tall. Speak with a full, deep voice. Be confident.

5. Encourage your dog to make eye contact with you. Look lovingly into your dog's eyes and tell him he's terrific. When he's rotten, give him "the eye," just as your teachers do when the class acts up.

6. When your dog acts rowdy and disobedient, use a command, such as the down stay, to calm him down and let him know you are the boss. Be sure he holds the command for at least twenty minutes.

7. When you are playing with Pastrami, once in a while, lift him up off the ground and hold him for a while. Or, if he's too heavy to lift, lift part of him and hold onto that for a while. This demonstration of your power will tell the dog that you are alpha.

8. In the wild, the alpha dog signals that he is top dog by grasping the muzzle of another pack member. You can send the same message by grasping your dog lightly over his muzzle. The submissive dog signals back by licking the top dog under its chin. So do not pet your dog under his chin. That would give him the message that he's in charge.

9. Always be kind to your dog. Work and play with a heart as large as a dog's.

10. The more you train, the more you play, the more you understand your dog, the more secure he'll feel, the more fun you'll have, the more comfortable you'll feel at the top—which is just where you belong, kid.

HOW TO SPEAK TO YOUR DOG

There are two ways to speak to your dog. The first way is to use short, simple words and always use the same word to mean the same thing. The dog will learn these words. When you call your dog, always say, "Pastrami, Come." Don't say, "Come here, Stupid," one day and "Get over here or I'll break your head," the next day. It just confuses the dog and gives the neighbors a terrible impression. If you want your dog to understand English, build his vocabulary slowly and stick to it. Make a list for your family so that they too will use the words he knows.

The second way to talk to your dog is to say whatever you like, whatever is on your mind, but don't expect him to understand your *words*. He will understand what you are feeling. You can scold him this way when he makes a mistake—as long as you do it in an angry voice. Or you can pour your heart out to him. Tell him about the bully at school or about the 42 you got in Math. He may even look as if he understands exactly what you are saying, and he'll be very sympathetic. Dogs are such likable creatures. Most of them are pretty good listeners and enjoy a heart-to-heart conversation whenever you are in the mood.

Encourage your dog to make eye contact with you.

45

Obedience Training

He could go to a special class for puppies.

WHEN AND WHERE?

The first question most people ask about dog training is, "How old should my puppy be before I start training him?"

You have already started to train Pastrami, by teaching him his name, the words *no* and *okay,* to ride in a car properly, to come when you call him, to behave when you brush him and not to growl over his food. For informal training, which includes all these everyday things, you begin training as soon as you get your puppy, usually at about eight weeks of age.

You can also begin to teach commands to your puppy when he's very young, starting a week or two after you get him. You can work right inside your house, in the kitchen or den, teaching sit, then stay, lie down and stay, come and stand. Work without distractions on these commands and work for five, then ten minutes at a time. This is a terrific way to lay the foundation for the more formal lessons in this chapter.

Formal lessons should begin when your puppy is five or six months old. You can start everything except the heeling indoors, but now that the puppy is older and his concentration is better, you will also train outdoors. You will start the heeling outside on a quiet street and then work your puppy in busier places, gradually adding in distractions to your training program. By the time your pup is six months old, he can work for at least a half an hour—and pretty soon, for a full hour. At six months of age, he is old enough to go to a training class and learn his commands along with other dogs, should you choose to train him in this way. Or, if you want to take him to school before six months of age, he could go to a special puppy class, sometimes called puppy kindergarten training.

Now you know when and where: before six months of age, informal training for short periods of time right at home or in a puppy kindergarten class; after six months of age, formal training out of doors and away from home or in an obedience class with other dogs. Now we can begin Pastrami's lessons.

LESSON ONE: HEELING

Check your slip collar and make sure that when Pastrami is at your left, the side of the collar that you attach the leash to comes toward you over his neck. Now place him in the heeling position: sitting at your left side with his head and neck even with your body. When you are standing still, he should be sitting squarely at your left. Sitting squarely means facing the same direction you do and sitting straight. To get him to sit say "Sit," pull straight up with the leash and push down on his rump, all at the same time. See—he's a genius. Whoops, he's up. Try it again. Soon he will learn to sit when you say "Sit."

Always begin heeling from this basic position. Say "Pastrami, Heel" and begin walking. Pastrami must keep pace with you, not you with him. When he lags behind or darts ahead, jerk him back into position with a quick tug, release on the leash and say "Heel." When he's in the right place, tell him he's a good dog.

At this point, old Pastrami doesn't have the foggiest idea of what's going on or what you expect. And it's his very confusion that will make him look to you to get answers. However, if he can't make a mistake, he won't learn. Dragging him around is not the answer. Give him enough slack on the leash to get ahead of you or behind you. Then be very clear when you correct him by jerking the leash and at the same time telling him "Heel." Be patient, but be firm. He has to learn how to learn since he's never been to school before.

In the beginning, whenever you stop heeling, tell Pastrami to sit and make him sit. He will learn to sit without being told whenever you stop walking. This accomplishment is called the automatic sit and you'll find it used in other lessons, too. Walk around with him heeling, make right and left turns, and stop every few minutes to practice getting him to sit. See that he sits straight and then praise him. Pull him right into your leg like a little hug to praise him. By praising him just where you want him to be, you encourage him to favor that spot. Then everybody's happy.

Now when you heel, try to remember to start and stop with your left foot. It won't make you walk any better, but it will help your dog's heeling a lot. It's easier for him to follow the foot and leg closest to him. If you stop on your right foot, he'll keep going a bit until he realizes you've stopped. So, give him the extra help he needs.

Your dog will learn to pay close attention to you when the two of you are working. He will especially keep an eye on your left leg so

Heeling

To get Pastrami to sit, pull up on the leash, push down on his rump.

Now begin in the heeling position.

He must keep pace with you.

Tug and release the leash quickly to correct poor heeling.

When you stop, Pastrami must sit.

Praise him warmly for a straight sit.

that he knows when you are going and when you are stopping. Paying attention not only makes him heel better, but it makes him look devoted and alert.

Heeling will take a lot of practice. Whenever you walk your dog, give him a loose leash going out so that he can attend to his needs, and heel him on the way back. Pretty soon he'll catch on and won't need to be corrected very often. But be sure you remind him to do the right thing when necessary while he's learning. It will pay off sooner than you imagine.

LESSON TWO: SIT STAY

With your dog in the heeling position, give him the command "Sit." Extend your left arm forward, hand flat, fingers together, palm down. Now swing your hand slowly toward your dog, stopping just short of touching his nose, and give the command "Stay." Step forward slowly with your right foot and turn so that you are standing in front of your dog, facing him. If he breaks the command by getting up or lying down, say "No, Sit, Stay," in a very firm voice and put him back *in the same spot.* When he seems steady, back away one step at a time to the end of the leash. Wait a few seconds. Now you can walk back to your dog. Return to the heeling position by walking around to the right and coming around behind your dog so that he is once again at your left side. As you approach him, hold the leash to the left and begin to gather it up as you get closer. At no time can he get up until you are back to the heel position and you praise him.

Did you notice that you were asked to leave your dog on your *right* foot? When he is coming with you, leave on the left foot. When you are leaving and he is staying, leave on the right foot. After a while, he'll get so clever at following these extra clues that he will stay or go according to what foot you leave on, even if you don't say a word. But that's after a lot of practice,

Build your dog's confidence slowly. Once he is steady in a stay, you can walk away quickly or walk around him and he will stay put. Eventually you can lengthen the leash with a piece of rope and get farther away from him. After a while, he will stay for a few minutes off leash and then even when you are out of sight.

Sit Stay

Stand in front of Pastrami, facing him.

Stay!

If he breaks, say "No, Sit, Stay," placing him back in the same spot.

When he's steady, do a stay from six feet away.

Walk around him and back to the heeling position.

Once he's caught on to the idea of stay, ask a friend to make some noise in the next room, to bang on the piano or slam a door. If Pastrami breaks, correct him and put him back. He will learn that he is safe when he obeys you and that these loud noises, which would ordinarily make him jump, are not things that will harm him. Never break his trust by tricking or fooling him yourself. Let the distractions come from elsewhere. In this way, Pastrami will gain more and more confidence in you as his training proceeds and improves. On the practical side, loud noises occur unexpectedly anywhere you and your dog might be. It is important for him to listen to you in noise and confusion as well as in a quiet, familiar place. So have someone help you by testing him once in a while, and work Pastrami in shopping centers, parks and on busy streets, too. After some practice, you'll be able to take your dog anywhere and he will behave well.

ENDING AN EXERCISE

You should always end an exercise. If you don't break the dog from a command, he'll begin to think, "Well, I sat long enough. I think I'll go see what's for dinner now." He must understand that you and only you will let him know when to break and that you will also let him know when lessons are finished and it's time to rest or play.

To end an exercise, return to your dog so that he is in the heeling position, sitting straight at your left side. Give him the command, "Pastrami, Heel," and take two and a half steps: left, right, close with left. After he sits straight, praise him warmly. Remember, too, that his name means he is to move, so do not use it in praising him. You can say "Good boy," "That's a good girl" or "Good dog," but not "Good Pastrami." Use his name with moving commands such as heel or come, and not with stationary commands such as sit, down and stay. After a short while, hearing his name will alert him to movement and he'll be on his toes as you give him his command.

Another way to end an exercise or tell Pastrami that school is out is the informal way. In your brightest, happiest voice, tell him "OK." Will he get it? You bet he will!

LESSON THREE: DOWN STAY

Always get Pastrami ready for new work by practicing all his old work first. Fifteen minutes of heeling is the best way to start a training session. It lets Pastrami know that school is on and it uses up some of his endless energy so he can concentrate on the new work.

The down is best started indoors. So after Pastrami has his walk and fifteen minutes of heeling and a few tries at the sit stay, take him home. Now put him in the heel position and ask him to sit and stay. Then with your left hand, point right to the floor, bending your knees so that you actually touch it and say "Down." Most likely, nothing will happen. Once again, old Pastrami doesn't have a clue to what you want. Repeat the signal and command, but this time, as you do, gently slide Pastrami's legs forward until he is lying down. Tell him "Staaaay," and praise him softly. Enthusiastic praise at this point might get him to jump right up. So far, so good.

A dog usually lies down when he's pooped and ready for a nap. When you are training him, he'll probably be pretty excited. So lying down will be the last thing he'll want to do. Because of this, some dogs act spooky when you make them lie down. Some get upset or even angry. One little Dachshund I trained got so confused, she went to sleep. She must have thought, "If I'm lying down, I must be tired."

Try the gentle method for the first week to give Pastrami an idea of what you want and to let him know that it wouldn't be all that unpleasant to lie down. This method may even be enough to teach him the command. But, for most dogs, you could make them lie down gently until you're 95 and they would never obey the command on their own. Of course, this is the goal—that they lie down without being touched when you say "Down."

Now if you can do something Pastrami will really dislike to get him to lie down, he'll do it all by himself to avoid that "something."

Meany Method #1: With Pastrami sitting at your left side, point to the floor in front of him and say "Down." Now, don't take the ring that makes the collar tighten. Instead, slip your hand under his collar, grasping the collar as a whole, and with your arm as straight as a board, take a deep breath and push straight down to the ground. As you do this, repeat the command "Down." Miraculously, where his collar goes, Pastrami goes too—down. Tell him "Stay." Leave on your right foot and proceed to the end of the leash. Wait two minutes. Now return to him and finish the exercise as in the sit stay.

Down Stay

Gently slide his legs forward until he's lying down.

Tell him to "Stay" and go to the end of the leash.

Meany Method #1

Meany Method #2

58

If you practice, he'll soon lie down without being touched.

Meany Method #2: Tell Pastrami "Down" and if he doesn't lie down, draw the leash up short. As you tell him "Down" a second time, step on the loop of the leash with your left foot until he lies down. Hold your foot on the leash for a few seconds and tell him "Staaay." Continue as above.

Find the method best for your dog for this command. Remember, the softest method *that works* is the right one to use. Add this command to your daily practice. And don't forget to heap on the praise. Down is the hardest command for many dogs. It puts the dog in a submissive position and he doesn't like this. He'd rather be on his toes, feeling dominant. That is why this command is so very important. It is not only practical for things like waiting at the veterinarian's office or keeping the dog under control while you do a puzzle on the floor, but it reminds the dog in a rather gentle way that you, not he, are top dog. To sweeten the training, when your dog lies down, sometimes, instead of doing a stay, rub his belly to praise him. That may help convince him that lying down isn't so bad after all. In a week or two, he should be lying down without a correction.

Remember, the down stay is second in importance only to come when called. You can use it to keep Pastrami away from your friend Marilyn, who is deathly afraid of dogs, and again when Uncle Herb comes over in his white suit. Use it in the car or when there's a freshly waxed floor in the next room. Or use it to calm your dog when he's having the crazies. And if one of Pastrami's friends comes to visit and you want a little peace and quiet after a while, put them both on down stays for a few minutes. (If the other dog doesn't know this command, whip out this book and get to work.)

LESSON FOUR: STAND STAY

The stand stay may seem like a silly thing to teach your dog. But aside from the fact that it will make him look super-classy, it has some practical uses, too. You can use it when you brush him, when you bathe him and for photographs. If your dog is pedigreed and you decide you want to show him at dog shows, you will need this command for either breed or obedience competition. A breed show judges the conformation of dogs: how they are built, how they move, how closely they resemble the ideal dog of their breed as described by the American Kennel Club standard. It may look like a beauty show, and in a way it is; but it is much more than that, too. It is the way serious breeders judge the worth of their dogs. It is the way they learn to breed better, sounder dogs for pet owners like us to love. Obedience shows judge dogs on their performance of set commands, the very commands you are teaching Pastrami from this book. They are very exacting about what the dog must do and how he must do it. He must not only perform his commands with near perfect ability, but in harmony with his handler and in good cheer. If you think you'd like to enter dog shows with Pastrami, first check with the local kennel club to find out when the next show will be held, and then go and see what they are like. In any case, the stand stay gives a dog judge a good chance to look at each dog being shown. And it gives you one more opportunity to create a better, calmer, wiser dog. Remember, anything your dog learns makes him smarter.

To teach the stand on command, begin as usual in the heeling position. Say "Stand," and move forward with your left foot first as if you were starting to heel. Pastrami will follow that left leg and get up. Now, swiftly place your hand (the left is easier as it is closer to the dog) under your dog's belly with a light touch or, if you prefer, inside his right, rear thigh.

Did you ever notice that when dogs sniff and investigate each other upon meeting, the hind section is where they do most of that sniffing? The dog being investigated freezes. Your light touch near the rear of your dog will trigger his instinct to freeze.

Stay right where you are, hand lightly on your dog, and say "Stay." If Pastrami seems steady, repeat the stay command once more and step away. After a few moments, return to your dog as usual and end the exercise.

If you plan to enter Pastrami in a dog show, he's not supposed to move his feet while he is on the stand. If he does, gently tell him "No, Stay" as you put the paw back where it was. You can let him move his head to look around a little and he may wag his tail. But his feet must stay put. So, before you leave him on a stay, make sure he is standing squarely and comfortably. If his legs are crossed or in an awkward position, he will have to move or he may even fall over and land with a clunk! Try it yourself and see.

What if Pastrami won't stand? After all, you've been drumming sit into his hairy little head for weeks. If you have trouble, make your baby a cradle. Just loop the leash under his belly like a cradle to prevent him from sitting. Once he understands this command, of

Stand Stay

Gently place your hand
inside his right thigh.

If he needs time to get
steady, you can get com-
fortable, too.

A cradle will help to teach him
to stand.

Tell him to stay and go to the end of the leash.

Brush him while he practices his stand stay.

course you won't have to use the cradle any more. Add the stand to your daily practice and when Pastrami gets steady at it, after about a week, brush him when he's on a stand stay. In fact, you should make practical use of all the commands as soon as possible. That's what dog training is for.

You're certainly becoming a good dog trainer quickly. And did you notice that as your confidence builds, so does Pastrami's?

LESSON FIVE: COME WHEN CALLED

With your dog sitting in the heeling position, give him the command to stay. Leave him, stepping away with your right foot first, walk to the end of your leash and turn to face him. After a moment, call sweetly to him in a kind and encouraging voice. After all, would you come if your mom bellowed, "Henry, you get in here! Henry, you just wait until your father gets home!"

Call "Pastrami, Come," and gather up the leash as he does. Now ask him to sit right in front of you, just as he arrives, and praise him lavishly after he does.

What if he's confused? Didn't you just tell him to stay? Suppose he does, suppose he just sits there looking stupid? Fine. Then crouch down, extend your arms out to the side and with enthusiasm and affection, call him again—and again, if necessary. "Pastrami, Come, come, come, Good boy, Come." Now you've got him! Give that boy a kiss.

Of course, you want Pastrami to come and come quickly the very first time you call him. By bending down now instead of dragging him to you, you will make him love to come. A little tug on the leash once in a while when he's not paying attention is fine. Later on, if you decide to go to obedience trials, you will have to stand tall when you call him and he will have to come on only one command, with no tugs. But you can work toward that, getting fussier about his work as you go along. For now, we want this boy to come and come fast, for safety's sake. Here are some more ways to speed him up and get him to come with enthusiasm.

Come When Called

Call sweetly and give a gentle
tug to get Pastrami to come.

"Come, come."

Run backwards coaxing him
to run to you.

When you have Pastrami at the far end of the leash on his stay, call him to come and, as you do, start running backwards, away from him. There's nothing on earth that speeds up a dog better than running away from him. After a minute, stop and let him catch you. Then praise like mad.

You can also speed up the recall with a recall game. Get friends or family together. Now, spread out so that Pastrami can go between two people or back and forth in a circle of three or four or more people, depending on how many players you can round up for a game. One at a time, call Pastrami, bend down to get him running to you, pet him quickly and let him go on to the next person—back and forth, cutting across the circle, any which way. Keep the game fast. Praise a lot. Make it fun for all. It's a great way to exercise the pup, too. But remember to play in a fenced yard if your dog won't come reliably. We don't want our Pastrami running off in the middle of a game—or ever.

And remember, too, *never* call your dog to you for punishment. If he has to be corrected for a misdeed, go to him, put on the leash, march him to the pillow he tore up or the glob on the rug and then correct him. He should never associate coming to you with anything bad or he just won't come.

LESSON SIX: THE FINISH

When Pastrami comes and sits in front of you, what then? Everything you've learned to do with him starts at the heeling position, so now we have to get him back to your left side.

There are two ways to finish the recall: to the left or to the right. If you choose to teach Pastrami the left finish, he will have to make a little circle at your left side. This is a fine finish for smaller dogs. If Pastrami finishes right, he walks to your right side, around behind you and finishes up in the heel position at your left side. Bigger dogs usually need the extra room of the right finish.

Left Finish

Call Pastrami to come. With him sitting in front of you, say "Pastrami, Heel." What do you think will happen? Right! Nothing!

66

Always end with "Sit Front."

And big praise!

The Finish

Left finish.

A circle at your side.

Back to the heeling position.

For the second and last time, say "Pastrami, Heel." Now step one giant step back with your left foot, leaving your right foot planted where it is, and lead Pastrami out to the left in a little circle that ends him up sitting, facing front at your left side. Then step back with your left foot so that your feet are even and, despite the fact that you did all the work, praise your dog.

OR . . .

Right Finish

Pastrami has come and is sitting squarely in front of you. Ask him to heel. Draw your leash up short and ask him to heel again. This time step way back on your right foot, leading Pastrami around behind you. As he gets there, step forward again and swap the leash behind your back to the other hand as he goes around and back to your left side and sits. He's a little confused, so praise him warmly. Pretty soon he'll get the idea and start making the trip, left or right, all on his own when you say "Heel."

From now on add the finish to your practice sessions. Now you can "finish" the recall formally with the left or right finish or you can finish informally by saying "OK."

Right finish—your right leg goes back.

LESSON SEVEN: THE FIGURE EIGHT

The figure eight is not a new command. It is a way of testing and sharpening Pastrami's heeling ability. To set the stage, you need two objects, about eight feet apart. You can use chairs, friends or Swiss cheese sandwiches. Just make sure Pastrami doesn't eat what he's heeling around!

All you do is heel Pastrami around the two obstacles in a figure eight, as in the diagram.

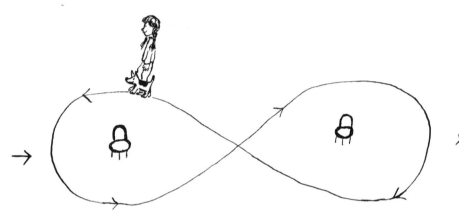

As you work, notice that when you are on the outside of the turn, Pastrami has to slow down to stay with you and when he is on the outside, he has to speed up. You, top dog, don't have to change your pace at all. Therefore, old Pastrami really has to be on the alert and use his brain. Correct him when he doesn't and praise him when he does. And don't do to many figure eights at once—you'll get too dizzy to eat those Swiss cheese sandwiches when the work is over.

Now is the time to warn you about sniffing because Pastrami is sure to sniff whatever you are "figure eighting" around. Should he or shouldn't he? Dogs enjoy sniffing things so much that some people think it's cruel to stop them. But this isn't the time for sniffing. If you want a well-trained dog, don't let him sniff when he's working. Sniffing will take his mind completely off you and his work. He should keep his eyes and mind on you and save the sniffing for his spare time. To correct him, jerk the leash and tell him "No sniff." If he is persistent, scuff your foot just under his nose as he sniffs, firmly telling him once more "No sniff."

If you both concentrate on each other, training will go better and faster.

SOME IMPORTANT TIPS AND REMINDERS
ON TRAINING

1. Be consistent and clear.
2. Remember to praise. That's what it's all about from your dog's point of view.
3. Train your dog all over the place. Don't end up with a living room champion.
4. Practice twenty to thirty minutes a day. Once a week, practice for one hour.
5. One dog, one trainer. That's you. Once he's trained, let the whole family in on it, teaching everyone how to give commands, how to praise and how to correct. Switching around while Pastrami is learning might only confuse him because each person would train him a little differently.
6. Don't start a new lesson until he's learned the old one. It will take him about a week to learn each lesson, but, of course, it will take a lot longer for him to learn to heel really well.
7. Never tease Pastrami or allow anyone else to tease him. This is good sense at any time, but it is particularly true when you are building his trust in you as his teacher and top dog.
8. Never use food with training, unless you are teaching a trick.
9. Don't quit unless you're the winner. Ending a practice session because you are having trouble will only make your job harder in the long run. Sure, there will always be that time when Pastrami just won't get something right. Fine. Simply go back to something he knows, have him do that, tell him he's the greatest and then quit for the day. That way, you'll both be happy to get back to work the next day.
10. If you're too busy, too late or too tired to enforce a command, don't give it in the first place.
11. Do the unexpected to keep your dog alert. Change your routines. Change your walk. Walk like a drunk. Walk in time to music. Break away during the heeling and run, calling "Come, come, come." Pastrami will have to pay attention if you are an unpredictable and exciting teacher.
12. Train with a clean choke chain. Tags or licenses can flip up when you make a correction. That could hurt your dog.
13. If your dog seems bored or too tired to work after only a few minutes, *don't be fooled.* Just think about what *you* do to try to get out of work.

14. Suit your corrections to the size, age and temperament of your own dog. Be extra careful with small dogs. Be encouraging with shy dogs.
15. Be responsible to your dog and your neighbors. Don't let your dog run round loose. And if your dog leaves unsightly messes around the neighborhood as you are training him, don't forget to scoop. (You can carry some plastic bags in your pocket or even tie them on to the leash.) In most places, it's the law.
16. Keep dog training fun—for you and for Pastrami.

The Spinach:

Some Nasty Problems and
How to Correct Them

JUMPING UP

Jumping up can be a big problem. If your dog is rude enough to jump on you when you walk in the door, he can knock you down, dirty your clothes, scratch you with his nails or squoosh the candy bar in your pocket. And grown ups usually think it's a poor idea, too. That may be because they wear white more often than kids do.

Curing your dog of jumping on people is tricky to do because some people are flattered when they get all that enthusiastic attention. They take it as a sign of true love, and not just bad manners. Often, in their pleasure, they will praise and pet the dog, thus reenforcing just what you are trying to eliminate. So step one is to inform them, though very gently, that Pastrami can love them just as well with four paws on the ground.

Since this problem is difficult to correct, you will probably have to resort to the element of surprise in order to convince Pastrami that you mean business. So I'm going to describe several ways to break your dog of jumping. Use any and all that seem appropriate to the size of your own dog.

The Bop

This is an old-fashioned method, but it can help if used rarely, as a surprise correction. Wait until the moment of your dog's flying leap at your chest, then jerk up your knee and bop him right in his chest. This method is supposed to discourage dogs from trying again. And for some dogs, it works. My dog Oliver, however, cleverly figured out that my knee only bent forward, and he began to jump on my side or back. This was more dangerous because I couldn't see the big lunk coming and so I couldn't even brace myself to hold up an extra seventy-two pounds. Hence . . .

He won't like jumping up any more
if he *has* to stay.

How to correct snoring.

Stuck Up

This time when Pastrami jumps up on you, grab his front paws as he makes his leap and hold him there—standing up. Don't miss the expression on his face. He won't like it any more if he has to stay. He prefers to bounce off your body a few times, leaving all kinds of yucky footprints on your school duds and even yuckier bruises underneath. But if every time he jumps, he gets *stuck up,* he'll think twice about his bad habit.

If your dog's tough minded and decides when you hold him up it's not a correction but an invitation to the dance, dance with him—backwards. That should help break this annoying problem.

The Slide

What if your Pastrami is cute and peanut sized? You won't be able to use the bop and you won't be able to hold him up or dance him backwards without needing a chiropractor when you're through. In this case, as he jumps, slide your foot in front of you, making him lose his balance and say "No" as you do this. The surprise should discourage him. Besides, little dogs often dislike it when their feet are touched. Your little dog can't get high enough to mash your candy bars, but he can scratch your legs, tear your mother's stockings or make little, bitty, muddy footprints on your clothes, so don't let an obnoxious habit go just because your Rin Tin Tin happens to be a small fry. And please don't skip . . .

The Best Correction for Jumping

When your big, klutz of a dog comes flying at you, as he jumps, slip your hand into his collar and jerk him sideways. Do not throw him. He could get hurt. Pull hard to the side and then ease him on down to the floor. Tell him to sit and stay. Now greet him warmly. In addition, whenever you are out and he tries to jump on innocent people in the street, jerk back hard with the leash and tell him "No jumping," then "Good dog" as soon as his feet are on the ground. Probably the worst jumping occurs when company comes. Before you answer the door, put the leash on Pastrami and when he sees who it is and those paws begin to rise, jerk back hard, say "No jumping!" and praise him the second those front feet touch the floor. Got it? Good. He will, too.

Of course, none of these corrections will work if you are not completely consistent. This means you must *always* correct your dog when he jumps on you or anyone else, and he must never be praised when he does it. It's not the kind of problem you can afford to fool around with—having some yes days and some no days. As you know by now, that doesn't work with dogs. So get your family and friends to agree to help. If Pastrami thinks everyone will correct him for jumping, the fun will go right out of this bad habit and he'll be able to give it up. You may have to share that candy bar to pay off your assistants. But so what! It's probably squooshed anyway.

CHEWING

Chewing is one of the worst problems people face with dogs. After all, how many couches can your parents afford to lose? In order to prevent damage while your pup is in the chewing stage (and the worst of this is six to nine months of age, after his adult teeth come in), you must use a dog crate. If you absolutely can't buy, build or borrow one, you will have to confine the dog. The trouble with that is that he can chew moldings, doors, floors or even walls wherever you keep him. So try to use a crate.

Starting when your puppy is little, monitor his chewing. Give him a couple of safe chew toys—rawhide, a nylon bone, a boiled knucklebone—and tell him "OK, Good boy" when he chews on these. When he's really young, he may move from toy to molding without seeming to notice that he did it. To a puppy, the whole world's a chew toy. Just bang your hand on the no-no, move the puppy a few feet away, give him a yes-yes and tell him he's terrific. Like a baby, a young animal needs watching.

Of course, you can't watch him every minute. You have homework to do and TV to watch. And you can't stay home and hold his paw all day. You've got to go to school. That's why you need a crate. When no one can watch Pastrami, crate him. Always make sure he's been fed, given water, walked and played with first. And please don't keep him crated for more than three or four hours at a time (except overnight, when necessary). The crate will help prevent disasters. But still, he's got to be out sometimes.

Continue to monitor your puppy's chewing for his first year. As he gets older, expect more of him. Now when he leaves his bone and begins to gnaw on the piano leg, grasp his collar and shake him back and forth, back and forth, just the way his mother did when he was a naughty little puppy (only she did it with her mouth). Tell him "No, Shame on you." Bang your hand on the piano leg and tell him no again. Then give him a chew toy and tell him he's terrific. If he goes right back to the piano leg, correct him again and put him in his crate. The message is: "You can't chew up my house. If you won't behave in my house, go sit in your house." Will he get the message? Trust me. After a time, he will.

Correct him when he's naughty.

Praise him when he's good.

Too pooped to chew is good.

Benjamin ©1986

New Paltz 8 mi.

Chewing is complicated. If you want to correct a chewer, you have to think about other elements that might be missing in the dog's life. For example, the dog might chew because he doesn't get enough exercise. That makes him anxious. When he's anxious, he chews. (So do people, only we do it on fingernails, candy bars and cookies.) If your dog is chewing, he should be getting out more—running with you, swimming, chasing a ball, going on hikes, getting trained, walking you to the store. Look at it this way: if he's too pooped to chew, he's going to be a good dog, isn't he?

Check out his training, too. Is it tight and snappy or sloppy and iffy? The more the dog sees you as alpha, the less likely he is to chew. After all, who's going to cross the boss? So, practice, practice. It helps all around.

Pay attention to your dog, but not without making demands on him:

- Brush him—but on the stand stay—while you watch TV.
- Practice his long down (thirty minutes) during dinner. That way he can be in the room, but he won't be a pest.
- Don't play games that encourage him to chew on or mouth his leash, a knotted up sock, your arm or hand. Play active, but don't play rough.
- Praise him when he picks up his toy to chew. Correct him when he goes for the rug or your sneakers.

With work and patience, this problem too will pass.

BITING

When a dog becomes a biter, the law steps in and all the choices of what to do are no longer yours. This one's as serious as they come and if you've read carefully and done your job so far, it shouldn't occur in the first place.

Let's suppose it does occur. Maybe the dog is genetically predisposed to being aggressive. In other words, he was born that way. Or maybe you just got an older dog who was raised by someone else who didn't train him properly, who didn't become top dog to him. He nips, he bites, he growls. What are you to do?

Kid, this is no place to fool around. If your little puppy growls over his food or nips you when excited, it's no big deal. Correct him with a firm "No" and, if necessary, send him to his room (his crate) for half an hour to cool off and think it over. But if your big, adult dog is growling and biting, it's not safe for you to work alone. Get your parents to help you: ask if you can take your dog to dog class or ask your parents to hire a trainer to come to your home. Most people have real trouble when their dogs become biters. Underneath, they feel that *they* did something wrong to cause it. But it's much more likely that it's a genetic problem. And if not, any mistakes made were not made on purpose. Sitting around and feeling guilty will not solve the problem. Working with the dog might.

With the aid of your parents, try the following.

1. Tighten all obedience work so that the dog obeys commands the first time they are given. Work the dog at least thirty minutes a day.
2. Increase the amount of exercise you give the dog. Sitting in the backyard is not exercise. He must run, swim, chase a ball. Anything happy and constructive will do.

3. Do not pet the dog unless he has just done something you've asked him to do. Do not let the dog bully you into constantly petting him. A dog who is fawned over in this way thinks he is top dog and that may be the cause of his biting.
4. Correct all signs of aggression. In order to do this, you have to know how to correct the dog safely. You can use the leash to shake the dog back and forth if he growls or tries to bite. After correcting him, put him in his crate for one hour. Another good, safe method is the use of a plant mister or water gun. Aim for the dog's mouth if it is aiming at you. I was once in a client's kitchen when the dog came at me with no warning. I had noticed a pot soaking in the sink. I tossed the pot full of water right into the dog's face and stopped him in his tracks. Then we confined the dog, cleaned up the kitchen and sat down at the table until we could stop shaking. So, be prepared and be creative. But remember, getting attacked by a big dog is no joke. *If you are already scared of your dog, get professional help.* If the aggression has just begun, follow the above suggestions for two to three weeks. If things don't get better, then get help.

One last, important, sad word on biting. If you have an adult biter and he can't be corrected, you mustn't give him away. The only sane thing you can do is to take him to your veterinarian and have him put to sleep. Then go home, cry your heart out and when you feel up to it, a week, a month or a year later, get another dog. With all my heart, I hope it never goes this way for you. But if it ever should, you've got to do the responsible thing.

OBJECT GUARDING

Here is an odd problem that belongs next to biting because it, too, is a problem of aggression. Some dogs fixate on an object or a type of object and when they get hold of it, they guard it with their lives. For example, a dog may have a special squeak toy or ball that he won't let anyone get near. Another dog may steal something weird like dish towels. Whenever he has a dish towel, any dish towel, you can't even get into the same room with him. You might think this is funny or just plain dumb. But what it is is dangerous.

If Pastrami hovers over a particular toy or bone and growls when anyone gets near him, the very first thing to do is to get rid of that object. Get the leash, call your dog, tell your mom or dad to throw out the object while you are out with Pastrami. If it's dish towels or something else he grabs that you can't throw away, make sure they are placed where they cannot be grabbed. Case closed? Not quite.

A dog who indulges in object guarding may be a troubled dog. There's a message in this madness. Something in the dog, something confusing to him, is not getting satisfied. Maybe that something is a genetic predisposition to guarding if the dog is a working dog or a herding dog or has these strains in his bloodline. Maybe he's just too aggressive and doesn't know quite what to do about it. Maybe the dog doesn't have a place and possessions of his own or enough privacy when he's tired. Maybe his training needs tightening or he's a big brute and needs a lot more exercise. These are the areas to examine.

If Pastrami begins this peculiar habit, remove the object forever. Just throw it away—and not when he's watching. Increase his exercise with positive, happy, active games—retrieving, jogging,

Remove the object he guards *forever*.

swimming. Check out his training. Is he obeying commands? Are you praising him enough? Do you correct him when he disobeys? Good. Does he have a crate he can retire to or at least a mat in your room where he can go when he doesn't want to be annoyed? Have you read about his breed? Do you know what work he was bred to perform and is there any way you could replace that work with something similar? Of course, your parents won't let you keep even a small herd of sheep to keep your herding dog busy and happy. But herding dogs love to jog. Running at your side, he'll feel useful. He'll herd *you* on your out and backs. He'll be in heaven. And what sporting dog wouldn't enjoy retrieving a stick from the land or the water? Carrying something back to you is what your sporting breed was bred to do and he's so nice, it doesn't even have to be a duck.

Last, but far from least, do you play tug-of-war with Pastrami, encouraging him to grab hold of something and struggle to get it and keep it with all his might? This kind of play is *always* a no-no. It encourages biting and object guarding. Replace it with positive work and positive play. That's a good dog owner!

Tug-of-war is a no-no.

EXCESSIVE BARKING

Barking is a different sort of problem from jumping up or chewing. Barking affects the neighbors, too. And so there is no choice involved in whether or not you stop Pastrami's noise making. You've simply got to.

Pastrami should bark when someone comes to your door if you live in an apartment or, if you live in a private house, he should bark when someone steps onto your property. But he should not bark for three hours every time a squirrel passes through town. And even when he is barking for a legitimate reason, he should quiet down after a reasonable amount of time.

To stop him from engaging in annoying and endless noise making, you have to catch him in the act of barking. There's no way to remind him of it hours after the fact. Once you catch him, you must do something that will make it not worth it for him to continue being a noisy pest. At first, a loud "No" will do the trick. When he turns to look at you, praise him. After all, when he turns to look, he has stopped barking.

If the verbal correction fails to do the trick, try banging on the door and then saying "No." That should get his attention. If not, try the shake. Grasp his collar and shake him from side to side. Tell him "Quiet" and if he won't take you seriously, put him in his crate for a while.

If he barks and barks when he's alone in the yard, maybe he wants your company. Dogs do not like being left outside all alone. They are pack animals and they like to be in a group, even if that group is you and Pastrami. Try to consider his feelings before you jump in with a correction.

But suppose it's not so much your company he's after, but your hamburger. Suppose he barks when you have a cookout, when he sees a bicycle pass, when a bird flies overhead or when a leaf falls. Suppose he's one of those. Try a verbal correction. "No!" Try a collar shake, back and forth, back and forth, like his mother did, and 'No, no, no." Try water. Catch him in his barking mouth with your water gun, saying "No barking. Quiet." Praise him when he listens.

Of course, you can't really expect a dog who's left outside alone to be absolutely quiet. Everything he sees will tease him into sounding off. Still, you'll have to teach him there's a limit.

And when your little barker is carrying on when he's inside, correct that, too.

Then think about *his* side of it. He's got a voice, doesn't he? And he wants to use it. So when you get the chance, turn to the trick section of this book and teach him to speak, count and add.

Meanwhile, don't forget prevention. When you leave him alone, always leave a chew toy. My little Japanese Shiba Inu, Lefty, plays ball by himself, like a cat. If your dog does, leave him a tennis ball, too. A busy dog is much less likely to bark. Prevention isn't just good dog training. It's great dog training. You can also give your dog something to look forward to so he won't feel so bad about staying alone that he barks his silly head off. Let him know that every day when you get home from school, you are going to play with him, let him romp and give him some exercise, a little education and even a treat or two. How can you let him know? Don't write him a letter unless he's one of those few who can read. (And don't think *that* trick isn't in the trick section, because it is.) Let him know by doing it. Be predictable. It will give you something extra to look forward to, too.

STEALING FOOD

You might think it's adorable when Pastrami steals food. Years ago, I had a crazy, red cat named Sasha. He was a master thief. If you were silly enough to leave a roast beef sandwich on the table, Sasha would spear the beef with one nail and slip it out from between the two slices of bread. He only needed a split second to leave you with a bread sandwich. He would also bite cupcakes on the run without ever slowing down. Good old Sasha. We still laugh when we think about his antics. But when a dog steals, it can get pretty unfunny.

Some dogs steal cupcakes from little children, which really depresses the little children. Others steal hors d'oeuvres from the table while the company is busy chatting. Some specialize in stealing defrosting roasts. It can be a big problem.

If you want to stop Pastrami from stealing, be sneaky. Set up the situation in which he steals. Then surprise him when he gives in to temptation. Peek around the corner and watch him try to get the roast off the table. As he grabs for it, yell "Nooo" and scare him off just as he is about to steal. But never let him actually get the food and win.

Sit at the table and gesture with a yummy chicken leg. When he tries to grab it, yell "No" and rescue your food. Do not reward him with a bite. He must learn that he can't eat or taste everything he sees.

If firm voice corrections don't do the trick, a collar shake will do the job. Prevention here, too? You bet!

- Don't feed him at the table.
- Don't indulge him with licks of your ice cream cone.
- Teach him that his food is dog food and that he'll find it, every day like clockwork, in his own dish on the floor.

Tempt him with a liverwurst sandwich and correct him when he gives in to temptation.

If your dog is housebroken, skip this section.

PROBLEM HOUSEBREAKING

I know what you're thinking. "We did this already." Right? I hope so. If Pastrami is housebroken, grin widely and skip this section. You can go right on to the wonderful tricks in the next section.

But some dogs are tougher than others for a variety of reasons.

Perhaps you acquired an older dog from the pound or a kennel dog who came equipped with a chronic housebreaking problem. Perhaps you gave Pastrami the run of the house before he was really ready and he's been secretly turning your furniture into fire hydrants. Or maybe he's trying his best but you're giving him too much water before he's completely trained or feeding him too late at night or making him wait longer than he's able. Use your noodle and see if you can figure out what's causing the problem. Now we can begin to solve it.

When housebreaking becomes a problem, it is handled much in the same way as puppy housebreaking but with a firmer hand and stricter rules.

First, you must use a crate. There simply is no other way that is guaranteed to get the job done.

Second, no run of the house. And that means absolutely no soft hearts letting Pastrami out and spoiling the difficult work being done with him.

We are no longer going to give Pastrami the chance to make an uncorrected mistake—that is, a mistake when he isn't seen. So when he's not with you or another vigilant family member, he must be in his crate. Confinement will force him to remain in close proximity to his error. He'll find that out if he tries it once. So don't give up on this cure if he does have an accident once or twice in confinement. Dogs are naturally discreet and clean and do not like to soil the floor if they can't leave the area fast.

When you feel like monitoring your dog, and that means observing him with a very watchful eye, have him with you. But make sure he can't sneak out of the room, leave a surprise for you and then return, looking like an angel. Don't get so absorbed in TV that you forget all about him. When you can't watch him or you won't be home, confine him to his crate. Make sure his walks are at a rigid and regular schedule and sufficiently long for him to relieve himself. Keep in mind that female dogs usually relieve themselves rather rapidly and all at once. Mature males, on the other hand, use their urine to mark territory. Each time your dog lifts his leg on a tree, post or hydrant, he's saying, "Mine." These scents become something like the Doggy News. One whiff on the local hydrant and Pastrami knows who's been around before him. He'll want to leave his "message" right on top of the last dog's message: "Not yours. Mine." And he'll want to hit as many trees, poles and hydrants as possible. That's just how dogs are. It is possible that Pastrami doesn't seem housebroken because you are not giving him enough time to relieve himself as is his need and pleasure. If you take a good hike with your dog of either sex, letting it sniff and relieve itself, you can then practice obedience commands and heeling on the way home, additionally insuring good housebreaking by reminding your well-satisfied pet that you and you alone are top dog.

Here are your tools for correcting problem housebreaking: a sane, rigid schedule; longer walks; obedience training; confinement and, if it's not summer, less water (for example, if your dog only goofs at night, take away the water bowl after 8:00 PM).

After a few weeks, try limited freedom for Pastrami—an hour in the kitchen with no one there. If the kitchen remains dry, increase his freedom, a little, tiny bit at a time. If there's an accident, correct your dog, walk him, crate him and clean up the kitchen. Only by being very strict can you completely get rid of this annoying problem. Keep trying. Stay tough. And don't forget those long walks. As your dog improves, alternate between confinement and freedom, increasing the freedom only when he earns it by keeping the house clean. Continue this procedure until you can give him the run of the house without fear of his soiling.

The Ice Cream:

Tricks, Activities and Games
for You and Your Dog

TEN WONDERFUL TRICKS
AND HOW TO SHOW OFF WITH THEM

What could be more fun than showing off a little with your dog? Some people say that tricks are not dignified enough for dogs, but most dogs love to clown around and get attention. Dogs don't think about dignity. They just like to have a good time.

Give Your Paw

Have your dog sit in front of you so that he is facing you and tell him to stay. Now say "Give me your paw" and as you say it, hold up your hand to receive Pastrami's paw. He might give you his paw, even without training, because to *paw* in front of him is a submissive gesture. It would be a way of indicating to you that he knows you are top dog. Most likely, he will just sit there looking adorable with all four feet on the ground. In that case, with your free hand, push him at the shoulder so that he just begins to lose his balance. This will bring up a paw. Meet his paw with yours and praise him a lot. He should catch on very quickly to this classic, endearing trick.

No matter how many tricks you teach Pastrami, this is the one everyone will try when they meet him. So, just as everyone made things harder for you when you were trying to stop him from jumping up and they were loving it, now everyone is going to help you. They will all ask Pastrami for his paw and be thrilled when he gives it. All this attention will give Pastrami just the positive reinforcement he needs to make him want to repeat this trick, over and over again.

Meet his paw half way with "yours."

Jump Through a Hoop

This is a grand trick, grand meaning good but also meaning large. And while it is rather easy to teach, you will never be able to convince anyone that your little dog, once he has jumped through a hoop on command, is anything less than a genius.

The best way to teach Pastrami to jump on command is to jump with him. Prop up a board in a doorway so that he cannot go under or around it. Put him on leash, take some room to get up speed and trot toward the board with Pastrami heeling at your side. As you near the board, say "Over" and step over the board with your dog. Give him big, big praise as you always do the first time he does something terrific and do it again and again and again.

It will take time for Pastrami to become a confident jumper so start with a low board and slowly build the height. Don't ever let him go under or around. He should think that the only way to the other side is over the top.

Soon you will be able to walk up to the board and tell him "Over" and Pastrami will take the jump without your company. Call him back and say "Over" again. Now he's got the idea and can make a round trip alone. He even likes it. Now it's time to start with the hoop. For that, a hula hoop will work very well. You may even have an old one in the house.

Place the hoop in the doorway so that Pastrami cannot go around it. For now, let it sit on the floor so that he can't go under it either. Get him used to the hoop by calling him through it and saying "Over" as he steps over the bottom of the hoop. Even though what he's doing now is no big deal, praise him when he comes through the hoop. It will all pay off later.

Once Pastrami is used to walking through the hoop, raise it a little off the ground, just an inch or two, and continue to have him come through it to you and give big praise. Gradually keep raising the hoop until your dog has to jump to get over it. Now when he comes through the hoop, give him a big round of applause. Now we're cooking. We're almost ready for the circus.

Once you are sure that Pastrami enjoys jumping through the hoop for hoots and clapping, you can take the hoop out of the doorway. Now, hold the hoop out to your side, not too high off the ground, and tell Pastrami "Over." He should go through the hoop. In fact, when you give the command a second time, he should come back

Measure him at the withers.

through the hoop. But what if he doesn't? Ask a friend to hold the hoop. Put Pastrami on a sit stay, put his leash on him and draw the leash through the hoop. You are now on one side of the hoop and he is on the other. Now call him and help direct him through the hoop with the leash. If he tries to go under the hoop, tell your friend to lower it. In fact, when you are holding the hoop, Pastrami may try to go under the hoop or around one side or the other. Any dog, given half the chance, will try to get out of work. But if you move the hoop, a little to the left or right, a smidgen lower, he'll get the drift. He's got to go through. You won't let him avoid it. Then, once he does, you tell him he's great. You love him up. You whisper in his ear. Well, in no time, he'll enjoy the very work he was trying to get out of. And it will show, too.

Whenever you want to do this trick, start out with the hoop lower than Pastrami is able to jump. Let him take a few easy jumps back and forth. After all, he's like any other athlete and he needs to warm up before giving the sport his all.

In addition, before you decide on Pastrami's maximum jump, you should make sure the height you have in mind is fair for his size. In order to do this, measure him at the shoulders (called withers in dogs) and then multiply by one and a half—that's your goal. That means a dog who is sixteen inches at the shoulder could jump two feet. Of course, if your Pastrami is old or not physically sound, you can keep the hoop much lower. The trick will look terrific no matter how high or low the hoop.

See if you can add some special effects to this trick. You can tie dozens of ribbons to the hoop so that they would stream out if you swung it. You can use two hoops, one in each hand, and have Pastrami go around you, jumping through one, then the other, and so on. Or you could use two dogs. Maybe some friends would want to get in on it and make up a little dog act, just for fun.

Take Food from My Mouth

This trick will thrill your friends more than most complicated ones. But if you have a nervous parent or an overenthusiastic dog, *don't try it.*

This trick requires control and gentleness on the part of the dog, so it is not a trick for puppies. Save this one for when Pastrami is about eighteen months or older. What you can do to prepare him is to make sure he is not snappy and grabby about his food. Never let him snatch things from your hand. When you give him a treat or a biscuit, have him sit and wait a second. Then be sure to say "OK" before you give it to him. Encourage him to take food gently and give him a stern "No" if he grabs.

This trick is one of my very favorites and it is so because it has two sides to it. In order to do the trick and not get hurt, you must have taught your dog a most important lesson—to be gentle, not grabby when taking food. However, when you do the trick, it appears to have no socially redeeming qualities to it at all. It looks stupid and daring. It will make people gasp, then giggle. Yet, because of its serious side, it's the smartest trick of the bunch. So here's how:

When your dog never fails to take food gently from your fingers, he is probably ready to take it gently from your lips. But in order to be absolutely safe, take a *huge* dog biscuit (the fattest, longest one you can find) or use a long-style bread stick, and place one end of it between your teeth. Have Pastrami on a sit stay and not in a wild mood. Calmly tell him "OK, boy, Take it." Of course, he will. He's no fool. If he takes it gently (you're safe anyway because of the length of the biscuit), praise him warmly, but don't get him wild. Now try again.

Keep working with bread sticks or huge biscuits until you see that your dog will slip the food from your mouth, not grab it. When you are very sure of your dog, begin to improve the trick by using smaller pieces of food. Crunchy things like potato chips or pretzels are fun because as Pastrami bites, they will break and you will each get half. It's a fun way to share food. And if you proceed slowly and carefully, this is a great trick that will get you and Pastrami a lot of laughs and attention.

Of course, if you rush forward without proper preparation, you can be the first kid on your block without a nose, which is a whole different trick and one I don't recommend.

Catch!

As you read on, you'll see that Pastrami will *love* this catching trick. This time begin with a small-sized dog biscuit. Put Pastrami on a sit stay and let him smell the biscuit for a second, but don't let him grab it. Now stand a few feet in front of him and say "Catch it," tossing the biscuit to him.

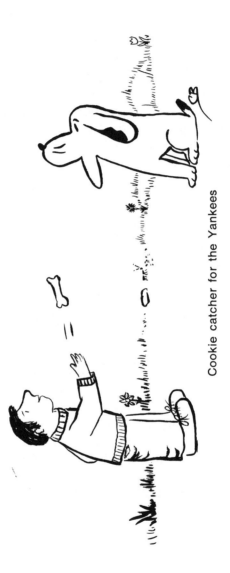

Cookie catcher for the Yankees

Most dogs find it easiest to catch if the biscuit is aimed just above their muzzle. But don't be surprised when Pastrami doesn't catch the biscuit, when he just sits there looking dumb and lets the biscuit bounce off his head the first few times. There's nothing to worry about. Just get him hooked on the game.

If Pastrami misses, he'll go for the biscuit. Let him. After a day or two, when he's catching pretty well or at least trying hard, don't let him eat the biscuit unless he catches it. (Are you catching on now?) This is a job for Speed Demon. When Pastrami's mouth is faster than a speeding bullet, he catches, he eats. When he misses, *you* dash in and rescue the biscuit. Say "Catch it" and throw it again. As you can see, Pastrami's motivation is all built in: food. But there's a surprise coming.

It's pretty obvious that you can get a little pig like Pastrami to work for food. But when he gets good enough to become cookie catcher for the Yankees, you will learn something interesting about dogs. You can now switch him to a ball and guess what? He'll love the game just as much. He'll enjoy the feeling of accomplishment, of winning. He'll feel great to be able to test himself and succeed. So who needs food in dog training? In this case, if you use a treat to get started, it becomes a kind of shortcut to getting your dog interested. But even then, when you switch the dog from food to a ball, he'll still want to play. In fact, he may like the game even more.

Food is a big distraction. Part of your dog's mind will always be on the food. Once you remove the food from the game, he can forget about eating for the moment and concentrate even better on catching and winning. In this case, his joy will come from learning and achieving rather than from eating. Ultimately, it will make him a better trained dog and a more clever one, too.

Now when you put Pastrami on a sit stay, let him sniff the ball, then back up and toss it toward him. Be patient. Use lots of praise. And watch Pastrami enjoy the challenge of catching a ball. When he catches, call him to come. Having been expertly trained by none other than you, he will, and he'll sit front. Now say "Out" and take the ball. You can even get him to move away from you with a "fake." Then tell him "Catch it" and start all over again.

Practice whenever you get the chance. This game is not only fun, it's good exercise, too.

Wag Your Tail

This isn't really a trick your dog learns. It's one that you learn.

If your dog will do a reliable stand stay, you've got it made. Getting your dog to wag his tail on command is just a matter of finding the right tone in your voice that makes him happy enough to do just that—wag his tail.

Some dogs are impossible because they never *stop* wagging their tails. Some dogs are shy and will wag in slow motion. In any case, this is a cute trick and worth a try.

Put Pastrami on a stand stay. Be firm and serious so that he stays put and doesn't wag his tail before you are ready. Now stand in front of him and ask him, "Do you want to wag your tail?" Don't just talk. Coo to him. Try to find the right voice so that his ears will go back in love and his tail will wag. You can say anything if the tone is right: "If you love me, wag your tail," or "If you're hungry, wag your tail." Be inventive. People will think you're a genius, and they're probably right!

Sleep

"Sleep" is merely a switch on another trick, one with the unfortunate name of "Play Dead." For our trick you'll need a prop, a small pillow that you can make, buy or find around the house.

Put Pastrami on a down stay. Gently turn him onto his side and place the little pillow under his head, reminding him to stay. Now place your hand on his brow, just over his eyes. Close his eyes as you say "Sleep, Stay, Good boy" in a quiet, soothing tone. If he takes his head off the pillow, put it back, saying "No, Sleep, Stay" and close his eyes again.

Be very patient. Work only after Pastrami's had a lot of exercise and is tired anyway.

When Pastrami gets good at sleeping on command, try dropping the verbal command. See if you can get him to do this trick when you give him his pillow. Then you can really have some fun by saying, "I think Pastrami looks exhausted, doesn't he?" and tossing him the little pillow. He'll lie down, put his head on the pillow and close his eyes. You can release him by saying, "OK, time to get up" or if you are musical, whistle reveille to wake up your little soldier.

Sneeze

Sneeze is a stupid trick and every dog should know at least one of those. (We'll teach Pastrami two.)

Watch Pastrami and see what makes him sneeze. Most dogs sneeze when they are happy, so Pastrami may sneeze when you pick up his leash to take him for a walk or when you get up in the morning. Begin by saying, "Good boy, Sneeze" whenever he starts to sneeze and sneeze right along with him. Sneeze and praise. Praise and sneeze. Good work.

In a few weeks, your dog will sneeze when you sneeze or when you say "Sneeze." Pastrami will sneeze. You'll sneeze. Achoooo. He'll sneeze. You'll sneeze. And so on. Stupider than this you can't get. Except for the next trick. You'll see.

Bump My Hand

Practice this dumb trick outside when your dog is very excited. The object is to try to get him to jump up and bump your hand with his head. Most dogs jump around when you first take them out. So hold out your hand, palm down and excite Pastrami even more with words like "Come on, boy, Jump, Bump my hand. Yeah, Good boy, Bump my hand." Go nuts when he does it, even if it's an accident. The nuttier you get, the nuttier he'll get, the higher he'll jump and the more he'll bump. Stupid trick? You bet. And now for the smart one!

Speak, Count, Add

This amusing trick will not only win you the admiration of family and friends, but also will help you with your math.

Your first job is to teach Pastrami to speak on command. This can be done by conditioning him to bark when you snap your fingers or clap if you can't snap—some people just can't. Just watch Pastrami and find out what makes him bark. Try showing him a biscuit, running back and forth or use the old reliable, someone knocking at the door. (You can always use one of those squooshed candy bars to bribe a friend to help you.)

Teach Pastrami to read.

Do this every day for just one or two minutes at a time. Once Pastrami will bark to your clap or snap, you can do the following snappy trick. Say your pup will count to five. As you say, "Pastrami, Count to five," snap your fingers. *You* count, but silently. After the fifth bark, immediately praise Pastrami—before he has a chance to bark the sixth time. Get it? Luckily, no one else will. They'll be dazzled.

Now it's time for higher mathematics. Tell your friends that Pastrami can help them with their homework. And give him a problem, such as "How much is two plus four?" Of course, you've got to know the answer, so don't make it too tough unless you have one of those miniature calculators hidden in the palm of your hand. Now snap and Pastrami will add. When he gets to six (guess who has one of those miniature calculators hidden in the palm of her hand!), tell him he's terrific and pet him. That's his cue to stop barking.

You can ask Pastrami any question that would be answered by a number and make everyone think he's a mathematical wizard. Try "How many legs does a cow have?" or "How old am I?" You can have lots of fun with this trick while practicing adding in your head. Your math teacher might even want Pastrami to come to school and demonstrate.

Years ago I taught my little dog Jody all his commands in French. My college French teacher asked me to bring him to class and show everyone how clever he was at a foreign language. It was great fun and I felt very proud of my dog.

And this reminds me of the next trick, a winner.

The World's Best Dog Trick

Now you are ready to teach Pastrami to read. First make a large sign that says: WAG YOUR TAIL. Next tell everyone that you have taught Pastrami to read. Imagine their surprise! When they beg you to demonstrate, put Pastrami on a stand stay and show him the sign as you use your friendliest voice to say, "Here, Pastrami, Read this sign."

And guess what Pastrami will do! Right. He'll read.

If your family speaks another language—or if your dog is a German Shepherd, a French Poodle, an Italian Greyhound, a Finnish Spitz, a Chinese Crested or a Japanese Shiba, find out how to write *wag your tail* in that language and make another little sign.

Now you can tell everyone you taught Pastrami to read German, French or Japanese. Show Pastrami the new sign and say "Can you read this, boy? That's a good boy. Take your Time. Good dog." And guess what Pastrami will do! Right. He'll translate.

And now you and your dog know the world's best dog trick. Kiddo, you two are terrific.

TRICKS ARE FOR KIDS

The whole idea behind tricks is to have fun and build your own self-confidence. Sometimes it's difficult to feel terrific about yourself or to feel important. Dog training and dog tricks will build Pastrami's confidence and yours, too. These are ways to accomplish something wonderful and real by using intelligence, patience and hard work. You have a right to be proud. So don't be shy about showing off and feeling great. You've earned the right by doing such a fine job with Pastrami. And he'll get a thrill out of all the attention, too.

ACTIVITIES AND GAMES

Draw Me!

Did you ever see those matchbook covers that asked you to draw something to see if you were talented enough to go to art school? Talented or not, Pastrami can help you to draw—him.

By using your dog as a model and by using your hands to feel the "lines" of his body, you will be able, with practice, to improve your drawing.

At first, try drawing your dog when he's still, on a sit stay or asleep. Later, when you get confident, you can try pictures of him on the go, chasing a ball or swimming in the pond. Don't be afraid to try again and again, to erase, to improve, to check the feel of a foot or an ear and redraw where you were inaccurate. Drawing your dog will help you to appreciate his beauty.

Business Is Picking Up

Suppose you are an older kid, not seven or eight but ten or eleven or even older. You might want, more than anything, to earn some pocket money.

You can start a dog exercise business. You can make a flyer for all your neighbors announcing that for a small sum, you will walk their dog, taking him for a long hike once a day so that he gets his exercise. Lots of people want their dogs to have a good, long excursion every afternoon, but they are away at work and just can't do it themselves. Older people sometimes have trouble giving their pets the exercise they need. Your service could be a great help to your neighbors— and to your neighborhood if you remember to pick up after your customers. In many towns, it's the law.

Now your good time with dogs will help you get strong legs and earn money.

He's getting used to the water.

A Ducky Game or Two

Summer is for being lazy, for spending the day doing next to nothing. It's for lying on your back and looking at the sky, reading a good book under a tree, hanging out at the local lake with the family dog.

When you and Pastrami go to the lake, you might like to give *him* some extra exercise with a ducky game or two.

Many reluctant swimmers will swim for food. Did you know that bread floats, at least for a while? If Pastrami is a reluctant bathing beauty, let him sniff a small piece of bread, then toss it just a short way into the water. Pastrami will probably walk in and grab it. Then he'll stand right there, up to his knees in water, and eat it. You know Pastrami!

That's fine. He's getting used to the water. Each time, toss the bread a foot or so farther. If your Pastrami likes food the way my Pastrami does, he'll be swimming in no time.

Once Pastrami likes to swim, you can teach another game. First, switch from bread to a stick. When Pastrami goes for the stick, cheer for him and clap your hands. Make just the biggest fuss when he brings it back to you. After a week or so, when Pastrami is on the way back with one stick, toss a second one and tell him, "Fetch, Pastrami, Good dog." Many dogs will retrieve two sticks at a time. See if Pastrami will.

My German Shepherd, Scarlet, has picked up three, jamming all of them into her mouth and sort of pushing them back to shore. When Pastrami retrieves, one, two or three sticks, clap for him when he makes his finds and keep clapping as he comes in. That's our boy, Pastrami!

Running Bases

Choose two spots, as far away from each other as you like, and mark them with pillows if they are indoors or sticks if they are outdoors. Now you and Pastrami can race back and forth between the bases. You'll be amazed at how fast he catches on and beats you to the next base. My Shepherd even learned to fake me out. She'd start to run to one base, then whip around and double back to the last one. That Scarlet, she'd even cheat to win.

115

By the way, this is one place where the dog can and should win. In training, you always have to come out on top. Here the dog almost always comes out on top. After all, he's got twice as many legs as you do!

Find It

This is my favorite dog game. You can start with a dog biscuit and easy finds. Put Pastrami on a sit stay, show him the dog biscuit and tell him "Smell it" (but don't let him grab it and eat it). Then set the biscuit on the floor a couple of feet in front of him, wait a second or two and say "Find it. Good boy."

Of course Pastrami will find it. He could see it all along. And for the first week, he should see where you hide the biscuit each time. Then, when he's hooked on this great game, hide the biscuit just out of sight, in the next room or in the hall.

Once your dog gets good at this game, you can hide a ball or a toy. It doesn't always have to be food. Now hide the object behind a potted plant, on the bottom shelf of the bookcase, sticking out of your shoe, and eventually, on a table, on a chair, in your pocket. As long as Pastrami is sniffing and searching, praise him and go wild when he makes his finds.

If Pastrami gives up, it merely means you've gone ahead too quickly, so back up and do some easy ones until you're sure he's ready for the more difficult searches.

This is a game dogs love and if you play it for company, they will find it both instructive and entertaining.

The Best of the Best

The best time you can have with your dog is almost always a quiet time. Dogs are wonderful companions for long walks, long sits, long waits, long anythings.

When I was a kid, my favorite thing to do was take my dog to the beach in winter. I lived just two blocks from the ocean and almost every afternoon after school, I'd take my dog to the deserted beach and we would walk on the cold, hard sand. I always loved the way our footprints looked on the sand, a long trail of them, his and mine, crossing and recrossing as far as the eye could travel. I always felt terrific after a hike on the beach with my dog.

Taking hikes or sitting quietly and reading with your dog at your side, these are good activities, too. Tricks are flashy and fun. And it's perfectly fine to show off with your wonderful dog and make people laugh. But the very best times are often those private times when it's you and your dog and nobody else.

Dogs love your company no matter what. It's great to have a dog for a friend.

It's great to have a dog for a friend.

Careers in Dogs

One of the most important and exciting aspects of your future will be the career you choose for yourself. You have seen by now how much Pastrami loves to work. And so will you if you choose something for which you are well suited. If you are truly an animal lover, a career in dogs might be very satisfying for you. Whet your appetite on these brief descriptions and then thoroughly investigate the one that appeals to you most.

Veterinarian

You might think that all you need to be a veterinarian is an abiding love of animals. That's only one factor of many. The vet is a doctor, a scientist, a lab technician, a surgeon, a businessperson, an employer and a master of tact. Vets must be able to deal well with people since animals do not come for treatment by themselves. They shouldn't be overly squeamish about surgery or euthanasia which is sometimes necessary when dealing with animals. You should be energetic because hours tend to be long and there are emergencies at all hours. And you'll need to be compassionate towards both pets and their concerned owners.

Veterinary Technician

Veterinary technicians assist the veterinarian with a heavy workload. They do laboratory work, x-ray, assist in surgery and medicate the animals. They do not diagnose sick animals, prescribe their medication nor perform surgery. Some universities now offer a degree in this field, with a choice of a two or four year course of study.

Dog Trainer

Dog trainers spend a lot of time dealing with problems of dogs and people, so the trainer must have insight about both human and animal behavior. It is hard work, mostly outdoors, and requires patience, understanding of animals, tact and self confidence. You will meet a lot of nice people and a lot of terrific dogs. Competition is keen and the work tends to be seasonal. If you love dogs, get along well with people and have an independent spirit, this might be for you.

Dog Groomer

Many breeds of dogs need special attention to look their best and go regularly to the groomer for "the works." Groomers bathe dogs, clip their nails, trim their coats to perfection and get rid of nasty fleas. They help owners to keep their dogs looking and feeling good. Groomers need to know the ideal standards of all the breeds they clip. A talented groomer can make a dog look leaner or leggier or more square by the way the hair is trimmed. Good grooming can work wonders.

Guide Dog Trainer

This is a rewarding field but with very limited openings. Guide dog trainers teach dogs to lead the blind. They work about two-thirds of the time with the dogs alone and one-third with the blind students and their new guides. So they must be patient and have a good hand with dogs as well as being compassionate and good with people. The hours are long and the work is tough but it is a fulfilling career that anyone could be proud of. The best preparation would be four years of college, possibly including some work in animal technology and courses in psychology.

Dog Boarding

When his owners go off for a week in the sun, what happens to poor Fido? Often he vacations at a canine hotel, the boarding kennel. He will have a run all to himself, often a mat or a bed to sleep on, regular meals, usually of what he eats at home, and sometimes even music to soothe him while he anxiously awaits their return. Running such a business is another possible dog career. Often it is combined with a grooming service and even the sale of supplies for pets. If you like business, can deal with customers and don't mind a lot of barking, speak to the owner of the local boarding kennel to find out more about this career.

Animal Photographer

Being a photographer is competitive work and photographing dogs is difficult. But even though your subjects won't hold still, they do make wonderful pictures. Probably the ones you don't plan will be better than the ones you do. Animal photographers are needed regularly at dog shows all over the country. And some advertise that they do portraits of the family pet for Christmas or other occasions. If you are talented in this field you can do calendars, work with authors, do work in advertising or you can "invent" your own line of work—like making greeting cards and stationery with photographs of the family Newfoundland or Cocker Spaniel.

Dog Walking Service

Several cities have dog walking services which advertise in the local paper. This is a service you can offer now on a small scale. Perhaps in your own town there are people with long work hours who could use a reliable, ambitious helper with Fido's daily exercise. A test ad in the local paper will let you know if this is something you can begin to do after school. Make sure you can handle any transportation problem before you advertise, and think seriously about the responsibility. If you are good, news will spread rapidly and you will end up with more dogs than you can handle.

Nonsense:

Questions from Our Readers

What do I do when my dog messes on the kitchen floor?

Run away and hide. With any luck, your mom will find it and clean it up.

Is it true that dogs come from wolves?

Not all dogs. My dog came from a pet shop on 14th Street.

This is a picture of my dog Herbert. Can you tell me why he never barks?

Evidently he's weak from hunger.

How can I stop my dog from sleeping on my bed?

Sleep in *his* bed with him. It's just your company he's after.

Sometimes our veterinarian gives us medicine for our dog. How can I get him to swallow a pill?

Carefully wrap the pill in a pound of chopped steak and see what a good patient he'll be. (Or, if you're a cheapskate, you can use a little butter instead and that's no joke.)

My dog Suzie loves peanut butter. Is there any harm in letting her eat some?

No. Just don't expect her to bark for a while afterwards.

Is Chinese food okay for dogs?

No. They get hungry again in only an hour.

I am sending you a picture I drew of my dog. Can you tell me what breed he is?

I'm afraid you're in for a bit of a shock. . . .

Do dogs turn gray as they get older?

Why not just be grateful they don't get bald?

Dog going bald

What do you get when you cross a St. Bernard with a Chihuahua?

A dead Chihuahua.

Summer is coming and the whole family is dreading those itchy pests. Can you say a word about fleas and ticks?

Yeech!

How can I keep my Dachshund Gypsy off the furniture?

Cover all your furniture with Cocker Spaniels.

I like to take my dog shopping with me, but sometimes she misbehaves and embarrasses me in department stores. How can I stop her?

Tell her if she won't behave you'll take away her credit card.

When my parents have a party, our dog Ben likes to drink champagne. What on earth should we do?

With today's prices, switch him to beer.

Our dog Ben

Nine Fingers Malone

My Golden Retriever weighs seventy pounds, but he still likes to sit on my lap like he did when I first got him. How can I break him of this habit?

Stand up.

How can I train my dog Ernie to do the dishes?

I don't know, but when you find out, call me collect.

What do you advise for fleas?

Scratch. And, by the way, stay away from your dog. He might get them, too.

Is it okay for dogs to eat jelly sandwiches?

That's a sticky question.

Which is the easiest dog to housebreak?

That's easy. The hot dog.

Is it okay for a dog to eat bananas?

I wouldn't monkey around with his diet if I were you.

Who was the first doctor to practice acupuncture on dogs?

Nine Fingers Malone.

Sometimes my dog jumps on the table and tries to steal our food. What should I do?

Quickly get the footprints out of the mashed potatoes before your mother sees them.

How can I tell a Beagle from a bagel?

Spread some cream cheese on it and take a bite. If it doesn't bite back, it's a bagel.

WHO'S WHO . . . IN ORDER OF APPEARANCE

Lefty, Shiba Inu, with Katie (on front cover)
Scarlet, German Shepherd, and Lefty, Shiba Inu, with the author
Kreskin, Ibizan Hound, with Derek
Sounder, Labrador Retriever, with Vicki
Lady, Cairn Terrier, with Diana
Oliver, Golden Retriever, with Greg
Shauna, Siberian Husky, with Vanessa
Sheba, Collie, with Norman
Taffy, Toy Poodle, with Jill
Tasha, German Shepherd, with James
Samantha, English Springer Spaniel, with Wendi
Duffy, Bearded Collie, with Tom
Mai Tai, Shih Tzu, with Jeff
Angus, Otterhound, all by himself

Thank you dogs and kids!

Special thanks to the late Elsworth Howell, my first publisher, for encouragement, good advice and friendship.

My thanks, too, to Charles Wiesehahn for his wonderful photographs, to Victoria Halboth and Judith Nelson for their valuable comments at the start of this project, to Rick Tomita and Christine Eicher for the little Shiba boy, and to my sweetie, Stephen Lennard, who never runs out of the room when I say, "You know, I have an idea. . . ."